ARCHITECTURE IN THE SHOIN STYLE

Japanese Arts Library

General Editor
John Rosenfield

With the cooperation and under the editorial supervision of:

The Agency for Cultural Affairs of the Japanese Government
Tokyo National Museum
Kyoto National Museum
Nara National Museum

KODANSHA INTERNATIONAL LTD. AND SHIBUNDO
Tokyo, New York, and San Francisco

Architecture in the Shoin Style

Japanese Feudal Residences

Fumio Hashimoto

translated and adapted by

H. Mack Horton

Publication of this book was assisted by a grant from the Japan Foundation.

Acknowledgment is made to the Mainichi Shimbunsha for kindly permitting use of floor plans in its publication *Jūyōbunkazai*.

Architecture in the Shoin Style: Japanese Feudal Residences was originally published in Japanese by the Shibundo publishing company, Tokyo, in 1972, under the title *Shoin-zukuri*, as volume 75 in the series *Nihon no bijutsu*. The English edition was prepared at Kodansha International, Tokyo, by Saburo Nobuki, Takako Suzuki, and Michael Brase.

Distributed in the United States by Kodansha International/USA Ltd., through Harper & Row Publishers, Inc., 10 East 53rd Street, New York, New York 10022; in Europe by Boxerbooks Inc., Limmatstrasse 111, 8031 Zurich; and in Japan by Kodansha International Ltd., 12–21, Otowa 2-chome, Bunkyo-ku, Tokyo 112.

Published by Kodansha International Ltd., 12–21, Otowa 2-chome, Bunkyo-ku, Tokyo 112 and Kodansha International/USA Ltd., 10 East 53rd Street, New York, New York 10022 and 44 Montgomery Street, San Francisco, California 94104. Copyright © 1981 by Kodansha International Ltd. and Shibundo. All rights reserved. Printed in Japan.

Library of Congress Cataloging in Publishing Data

Main entry under title:

Architecture in the shoin style.

   Translation of Shoinzukuri, originally issued as
no. 75 of Nihon no bijutsu
  Bibliography: p.
  Includes index.
  1. Architecture, Shoin. 2. Architecture—Japan—
Kamakura-Momoyama periods, 1185–1600. 3. Architecture—
Japan—Edo period, 1600–1868. I. Hashimoto, Fumio,
1917– II. Horton, H. Mack. III. Nihon no bijutsu.
NA7451.S55813 1981   728.8′0952   79–91519
ISBN 0–87011–414–X

First edition, 1981

CONTENTS

Japanese Art Periods

Prehistoric		−537
Asuka		538–644
Nara		645–781
Hakuhō	645–710	
Tempyō	711–781	
Heian		782–1184
Jōgan	782–897	
Fujiwara	898–1184	
Kamakura		1185–1332
Nambokuchō		1333–91
Muromachi		1392–1572
Momoyama		1573–99
Edo		1600–1867
Meiji		1868–1912

Note: This table, compiled by the Agency for Cultural Affairs of the Japanese Government for the arts and crafts, has been adopted for general use in this series. In this volume, however, stylistic considerations call for slightly different dates for the Muromachi (1333–1567), Momoyama (1568–1614), and Edo (1615–1867) periods.

A Note to the Reader

Japanese names are given in the customary Japanese order, surname preceding given name. The names of temples and subordinate buildings can be discerned by their suffixes: *-ji, -tera, -dera* referring to temples (Tōshōdai-ji; Ishiyama-dera); *-in* usually to a subtemple attached to a temple (Shōryō-in at Hōryū-ji). Japanese names for buildings or rooms within buildings are sometimes generic, such as *tsugi no ma* (anteroom), and sometimes specific, as in Sotetsu no Ma (Palm Room). In this book, the former are italicized when used in their general sense and romanized with capitals when referring to a specific room bearing the name. Also note that the measurements appearing in floor plans are in meters.

ILLUSTRATIONS

INTRODUCTION

Natsugusa ya	The summer grasses—
Tsuwamono domo ga	Of brave soldiers' dreams
Yume no ato	The aftermath.[1]

While it is true as Bashō suggests in his famous *haiku* that temporal power is but a fleeting vanity, and that all who build and all that is built must eventually pass away, a few of the palaces and other residences from Japan's feudal era have outlived both their builders and their unsettled times to recall to mind even today the dreams and the actual accomplishments of their creators. Many of the structures are built in the *shoin* style, an architectural type first seen in warrior residences of the Muromachi period (1333–1567). The style was strongly influenced by elements of the architecture of the Zen sect, whose priests were closely associated with the military government of the time. From the early seventeenth century to the middle of the nineteenth (known as the Edo period), the *shoin* style was the standard for military mansions, temple guest halls, and Zen abbot's quarters. The nobility in Kyoto selectively adopted the style as well, though continuing also to build in the earlier *shinden* style, a type of residence used during the era of the court's ascendency in the ninth through twelfth centuries. As the Edo period progressed, elements of the *shoin* style were also adopted by members of the lower classes, and it survives today in the Japanese-style rooms of domestic structures. What we think of today as "traditional Japanese houses" are nothing other than later variations on the *shoin* residence.

As the author of this book shows in detail, this one style was thus made to answer the requirements of a number of different classes and life styles. That it has survived for half a millennium proves that it did indeed provide satisfactory solutions to the varied demands imposed upon it. In so doing, it evolved along two major lines. One of these, the standard *shoin* style, is represented at its most magnificent by the Nino-maru Palace of Nijō Castle (1624–26). The other is the *sukiya shoin*, a relaxed and per-sonalized combination of the standard *shoin* with various elements of the teahouse. The Kuroshoin of the Nishi Hongan-ji temple (1656–57) and the Katsura Detached Palace (*ca.* 1618–63) are two of the best known examples of the *sukiya shoin* style. These two types show the wide variety of effects attainable through the general *shoin* frame-work.

1. Ninomaru Palace of Nijō Castle.
The constituent buildings of the Ninomaru Palace are
laid out in a zigzag plan and recede diagonally from the
Karamon ("Chinese" Gate) and Kurumayose entrance
vestibule at the right side of the illustration. The ridge
alignment of the gray-tiled hipped-and-gabled roofs
alternates from building to building, with the gilt ornamentation visible on the gable bargeboards of the
buildings facing south—the Tōzamurai and kitchens
behind, the Ōhiroma, and the Shiroshoin.

2. Jōdan no Ma of the Ōhiroma; Ninomaru Palace, Nijō Castle.

The Ōhiroma is the central complex of the Ninomaru Palace. Reserved for the most formal audiences, it contains the largest Jōdan no Ma, for the shogun's personal use. The decor as well is in the most formal style possible, the pines of the great *tokonoma* and the shoots of bamboo on the shelf alcove being typical subjects for a space of this dignified nature. This is the only space in the complex with a double coved and coffered ceiling, and the individual coffers are decorated with brilliant polychrome designs. This interior decor, with its scintillating mural paintings and metalwork, is the paramount example of a warrior *shoin*.

The Ninomaru Palace (pl. 1) was begun in 1624 by Iemitsu, the third shogun of the Tokugawa military regime. At that time, the Tokugawa shogun had held un-disputed rule over the country for only nine years. One of the paramount requirements for official structures built by the shogunate at that time, then, was to symbolize the authority of the Tokugawa and give immediate and awe-inspiring form to the power they wielded. Rodrigo de Vivero y Velasco tells of this power in an account of an audience with "the Emperor" (in fact, the retired Tokugawa shogun, Ieyasu) that he witnessed in 1609 at Suruga:

> There entered one of the greatest nobles of Japan, whose high rank was evident from the gifts he brought—bars of silver and gold, silk robes and other things, all of which must have been worth more than 20,000 ducats. All this was first of all placed on some tables but I do not believe the Emperor even looked at it. Then at over a hundred paces from where His Highness was seated, this *tono* prostrated himself, bowing his head so low that it looked as if he wanted to kiss the ground. Nobody said a word to him nor did he raise his eyes towards the Emperor on entering and leaving. Finally he turned and withdrew with his large retinue, which, according to some of my servants, numbered more than 3,000 men.[2]

Certainly the original function of castles was fortification, and those of the Tokugawa had their full complement of mammoth stone ramparts, moats, and iron-studded gates, but major consideration was also afforded to authoritative appearance for its own sake. Of course, the aforementioned defense elements provided some of this in themselves, but the gold-appointed soaring gables and the graceful yet formidable roofs of gray tile did much to strengthen the impressive appearance of the exteriors. The degree to which decor itself contributed to the at once inspiring and intimidating grandeur can best be seen in the Ōhiroma, the most formal building in the Ninomaru Palace. It is the area of the structure giving the most uncompromising expression of power and magnificence, and shows the *shoin* in its most majestic form.

The main audience hall of the Ōhiroma complex is composed of two contiguous spaces, a raised section called the Jōdan no Ma and one a step lower, the Gedan no Ma (pl. 2). The height of this combined space, which we will call the Ōhiroma audience hall, is modest, being no more than three times that of a human being. From the point of view of mere area, the Ōhiroma audience hall is far smaller than equivalent chambers in European palaces. Alexander Soper, in fact, goes so far as to write in reference to an audience hall in another building in the standard *shoin* style that "the proportions . . . are those of a basement."[3] The pervasive horizontality of the space is emphasized by two unbroken frieze rails (pl. 3), one located a bit over head-height (*uchinori nageshi*) and the other at the interface with the ceiling (*tenjō nageshi*), and by the ceiling itself, which rather than lightening the area overhead as

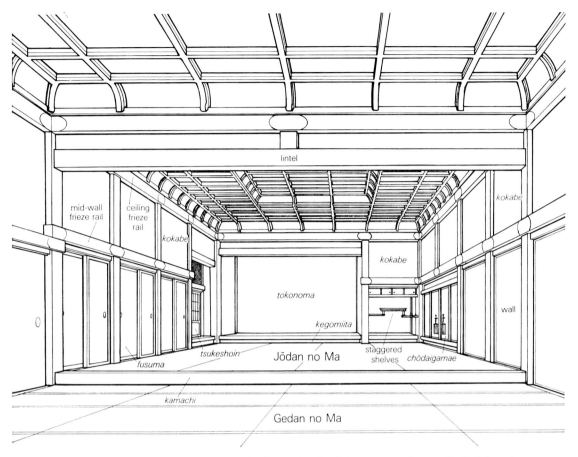

Labels in figure: lintel, kokabe, mid-wall frieze rail, ceiling frieze rail, kokabe, kokabe, tokonoma, wall, kegomiita, tsukeshoin, Jōdan no Ma, staggered shelves, chōdaigamae, fusuma, kamachi, Gedan no Ma

3. Example of a *jōdan no ma* in the standard *shoin* style.

would a white ceiling, clearly prohibits upward visual movement. The low ceiling and unbroken frieze rails emphasize the length of the room rather than the width or height and underscore the distance between the shogun on the raised-floor section and the lords on the lower, thus accentuating the shogun's superiority and inapproachability.

It is not the dimensions of the space but the way its surfaces are treated that makes the Ōhiroma audience hall one of the sublime moments in world architecture. The room is finished in gold and polychrome, its walls, screens (*fusuma*), and ceiling glistening even in the dim light from the southern and western verandas. The screens, with their metallic luster, seem solid and impervious, though being actually only of wood and paper. The mammoth pine trees, rendered on the gold background in bold strokes of brown and green, are at once decorative and powerful. They are the work of Kanō Tan'yū's atelier, and are in the tradition of Kanō Eitoku, who developed this monumental painting style to grace the halls of the earlier military leaders Nobunaga and Hideyoshi.

The bold exuberance of these brightly colored renderings is complemented by equally elaborate and costly detail. The joints of the wooden members are concealed by golden plaques, some figured with the three hollyhock leaves (*mitsuba-aoi*) of the Tokugawa family crest. The posts and frieze rails framing the panels are cut square

17

with narrow bevels on the edges, the square cut being a main characteristic of the *shoin* style. The sharp edges and smooth planes of these members contribute to the sense of rectitude and formality which characterized shogunal audiences. The coved and coffered ceilings are wonders of craftsmanship, with the grid of ceiling runners finished in glistening black lacquer with gold at the intersections and detailed polychrome designs pasted onto the ceiling panels themselves. It is said that 20,250 man-days were required for the construction of the Ōhiroma complex. The detail and precision of the ceiling alone makes this figure most plausible.

The Ninomaru Palace is one of the earliest examples of gold leaf and polychrome painting being used not only on the *fusuma* sliding screens, but on the *kokabe* (literally, "small walls") above that reach to the ceiling (pl. 3). The mammoth pines stop not at head height as was the case before this time, but extend to the very top of the wall, adding immensely to the heroic quality of the space. Hirai Kiyoshi theorizes in his article "The History of the Japanese House"[4] that the first painted *fusuma* came about as sliding versions of the free-standing screens (*byōbu*) used in the Heian period (782–1184) to subdivide interior space. The *kokabe*, the area above the mid-wall frieze rail, was left white, which Hirai theorizes struck the designers of the time as being tantamount to being empty and open. A narrow space (*arikabe*; literally, "ant wall") above the ceiling frieze rail was left white as well, and, more importantly, the posts were not allowed to visually penetrate this space, being instead plastered over to create an unbroken band below the ceiling. This caused the ceiling seemingly to float above the room itself. Despite the trend in the latter sixteenth century toward opulent architecture, represented most vividly in the building schemes of Toyotomi Hideyoshi, the *kokabe* continued to be finished in white plaster. Even the sumptuously polychromed audience hall of the Nagoya Castle Hommaru of 1615 (pl. 4), destroyed in World War Two, retained white *kokabe*. By comparison, the Ninomaru is overwhelmingly more magnificent. The Ōhiroma audience hall is no longer open at the top, and the ceiling does not float—rather, the space becomes a solid cube of gold (pl. 2). Hirai theorizes that this profound change had first occurred in another building constructed a few years earlier by Kobori Enshū, about whom we will hear much more in Chapter Five, and was then introduced into the Ninomaru Palace.

The Shoin of Nishi Hongan-ji temple also shows this "total decoration" concept (pl. 102). Until comparatively recently, however, both the Shoin and the Ninomaru Palace were thought to have been products of the Momoyama period (1568–1614). The Shoin in particular was held to have been originally built as part of one of Hideyoshi's Fushimi Castle projects. This theory led to the long-accepted conclusion that Japanese architecture reached the height of its splendor in the Momoyama period. It has since been shown, however, that the Ninomaru dates to 1624–26, and that the Shoin of Nishi Hongan-ji was not moved from Fushimi Castle but rather most likely built much later, in 1632–33. This means that at least two of the buildings formerly considered quintessential of the Momoyama period were ac-

4. Jōdan no Ma of the Audience Hall; Hommaru Palace, Nagoya Castle (not extant).

tually not built until the Kan'ei era (1624–44) of the Edo period. A building actually constructed in Hideyoshi's taste is seen rather in the Guest Hall of Saikyō-ji, which, it is believed, most likely *was* moved from Hideyoshi's first Fushimi Castle, at Shigetsu, after the castle was destroyed in an earthquake in 1596 (pl. 72). Its comparatively subdued scheme is immediately apparent. The inference is that it was in the early years of the Edo period and not the Momoyama period proper that Japanese architecture reached its most effusively ornamental stage.

The power of the Tokugawa shogun is expressed in the Ōhiroma audience hall of the Ninomaru Palace not only by the general opulence of the space but by several specific architectural elements designed to underscore his place at the top of the country's military hierarchy. One of these is the aforementioned separation of the audience hall into two constituent subspaces—the Jōdan no Ma for the shogun and the Gedan no Ma, functioning like an anteroom, for his vassals (pls. 2–3). This separation, which is sufficient to show clearly the difference in status between the shogun and the lesser lords but not so great as to obscure the essential unity of the combined audience area, is effected in several ways. The ceilings over the two subspaces are, for instance, treated differently. That over the Gedan no Ma is of a comparatively

19

simple coved and coffered design, whereas that over the shogun is a more elaborate double-coved and coffered type, which makes the ceiling area over the place where the shogun sat the highest in the hall. Separation of shogun and vassals is also emphasized by a lintel at the juncture of the two ceiling areas. The division between the Gedan no Ma and the San no Ma to the east is even more pronounced, with not a lintel but an entire transom (*ramma*) with elegant carving being used. The Ninomaru Palace also includes simpler, uncarved transoms, such as that seen between the Ni no Ma and San no Ma of the Kuroshoin (pl. 94). Furthermore, as we have seen, another division between the Jōdan no Ma and the Gedan no Ma is effected by the level of the flooring, that of the former being one step higher. Jōdan no Ma, in fact, literally means "Upper-level Room," and Gedan no Ma "Lower-level Room." Differing floor levels, coffered or coved and coffered ceilings, and transoms are all characteristic of the standard *shoin* style.

Variations in floor level in particular are the result of a long process having its roots in the Heian period (782–1184). In the *shinden* style of building, the type of structure favored by the upper classes of the time (see Chapter One), the floors were of polished wood. People sat on straw mats that were put in place as needed. Differences in social status were marked by variations in the size of the mats and in the treatment of their borders; costly embroidery was used for princes and ministers and a variety of less ornate designs down the hierarchical scale. However, Ōta Hirotarō relates in chapter three of his *Shoin-zukuri*[5] that during Japan's middle ages (roughly from the late twelfth century to the mid-sixteenth) some rooms had *tatami*, rectangular mats of woven rush, laid permanently around the periphery or over the entire floor. When this occurred, it became impossible to use individual borders on the mats to indicate differences in status. Instead, persons of high rank would sit in the rooms with *tatami* and their inferiors in rooms with none, the difference in floor height created by the approximately five-centimeter-thick mats constituting a type of *jōdan* or "upper level," according to Ōta. Still later, most rooms were covered completely with mats. It thus became impossible to distinguish social level according to whether a room had a bare floor or *tatami*. *Tatami* borders were still occasionally varied from room to room to indicate hierarchal differences, but this was not as visually effective as when each person used his own mat and both the top and side of that mat were visible. It thus developed that one room or part of a room would be built higher than the rest to indicate clearly the superior social position of those seated on it. This, Ōta theorizes, was the beginning of the *jōdan*. While there are examples of differences in floor level in earlier *shinden*-related structures, it is not until *tatami* were on all the floors that the main room came commonly to have a *jōdan* area. Complete *tatami* floors are another feature of the *shoin* style. The *jōdan*, *tatami*, and polychrome paintings figure prominently in Richard Cocks's description dated 1616 of Edo Castle under the second Tokugawa shogun, Hidetada (the "Emperour" in the account):

The Emperours pallis is a huge thing, all the rums being gilded with gould, both over head and upon the walls, except som mixture of paynting amonst of lyons, tigers, onces, panthers, eagles, and other beastes and fowles, very lyvely drawne and more esteemed then the gilding. . . . [The Emperour] sat alone upon a place somthing rising with 1 step, and had a silk *katabira* of a bright blew on his backe. He set upon the mattes crossleged lyke a telier; and som 3 or 4 *bozu* or pagon pristes on his right hand in a rum somthing lower. Non, no not Kōzuke *Dono*, nor his secretary, might not enter into the rowme where he sat . . . all the rowmes in his pallis under foote are covered with mattes edged with damask or cloth or gould, and lye so close joyned on to an other that yow canot put the point of a knife betwixt them.[6]

But the elements of the Ōhiroma audience hall at Nijō Castle which most strikingly indicate the area of central importance (pls. 2–3) are the decorative alcove (*tokonoma*) on the far wall of the Jōdan no Ma, the staggered shelves (*chigaidana*) on its immediate left, the desk alcove (*tsukeshoin*) on the veranda wall to its right, and the decorative doors (*chōdaigamae*) on the wall to its left. In this hall these four interior fixtures, which are the most immediately recognizable elements of the *shoin* style, are seen in their mature forms and locations.

The most conspicuous of the four is the decorative alcove, or *tokonoma*. Its back wall is decorated with an immense and aged pine that is located at the mid-point of the wall and bends toward the light of the veranda to form a majestic visual frame for the seated shogun. Due to the large size of the *tokonoma*, it is also known as an *ōdoko* ("great *tokonoma*"). This element has had the greatest longevity of any of these four *shoin* fixtures, and it is still found in many Japanese homes in much abbreviated forms. The *tokonoma* is simply an alcove with a floorboard at the base raised a short distance above the *tatami*, and with a lintel at the top, set above the level of the mid-wall frieze rail.

Itō Teiji relates that the word *toko* in the Kamakura (1185–1332) and Muromachi (1333–1567) periods referred not to a decorative alcove but rather to a raised floor or bench where a person could actually sit.[7] This form was preserved with variations in the later narrow and deep *tokonoma* alcoves of teahouses. A much more direct source of what we now know as the *tokonoma*, though, was developed, in the Muromachi period, primarily as a place to display the hanging scrolls which were being imported from China at the time. Contemporary illustrations also show the space decorated with the *mitsugusoku*, the three standard ornamental fixtures consisting of incense burner, flower vase, and candle stand. In this early period the space was known as the *oshiita*. Wide and shallow, it had a thick lintel and a thick floorboard made of a single, solid plank and was separated from the *tatami* level by a narrow wall space called the *kegomiita* (pl. 3). In the Momoyama period (1568–1614) the space came to be called the *tokonoma*, and designs became increasingly varied as influences from teahouse architecture were selectively introduced.

On the side of the *tokonoma* further from the veranda are the staggered shelves (*chigaidana*), those of the Ninomaru Ōhiroma audience hall being built in the *seirō-dana* configuration with the central shelf section raised above the two flanking shelves, which are slightly staggered in height (pls. 2, 5). Shoots of bamboo, symbolic, like the pine, of durability and longevity, spring forth from the corner of the alcove and droop both above and below the shelves, harmonizing in their slenderness with the delicacy of the alcove woodwork, where a continuation of the pine motif of the *tokonoma* might have been obstrusive. Above the shelves, at the top of the alcove, are cabinets with two sets of narrow sliding panels decorated with four types of flowers and black lacquer frames jointed with unerring precision. The height of the alcove is determined by the level of the mid-wall frieze rail, which unifies the back wall with the sides. The cupboards and alcove are aligned carefully with the upper and lower runners of the decorative doors (*chōdaigamae*) at the side, again bearing witness to the forethought with which every element in the Ōhiroma audience hall was designed and to the elegant precision with which the designs were carried out.

The shelves are believed to have developed from the movable shelves used in the Heian period (782–1184). Eventually, they came to be built-in, the earliest extant example of the fixed variety being found in the Tōgu-dō at the Higashiyama Villa of the shogun Ashikaga Yoshimasa, dating to 1485 (pl. 29). As in the case of the *tokonoma*, early illustrations have survived of these shelves; from them it appears that the shelves were originally used for storage of reading matter and writing implements. Written records, however, show that at an early stage the decorative possibilities of these shelves were being exploited, and Yoshimasa himself is recorded as asking the opinion of a monk learned in such matters as to which books should be displayed there. As time went on, the number of shelf styles increased greatly; standard manuals from the Edo period commonly list nearly fifty varieties. The most famous shelf styles, known as the "three supreme shelves," are discussed in the text.

The shelves were, in Yoshimasa's time, located next to the reading and writing desk, the *tsukeshoin*, a position sensible from a functional point of view. By the time the Jōdan no Ma of the Ninomaru Ōhiroma audience hall was constructed a century and half later, however, the shelves were most often located across the room from the desk (pl. 2). But the *tsukeshoin* alcove was still built into the veranda wall, so as to take advantage of the direct light from that side. The audience hall example here is composed of a floorboard/writing surface unified in height with the floorboard of the *tokonoma* on which it abuts at right angles. The back of the alcove is made up of four sliding wainscoted paper screens (*shōji*) with delicate latticework. These can be opened at will to allow sunlight to stream in directly. Their upper ends fit into a continuation of the mid-wall frieze rail which again provides unification of room design. A delicately carved transom fits above this frieze rail and below the alcove ceiling, this ceiling located in height exactly halfway between the mid-wall frieze rail

5. Staggered shelves of the Jōdan no Ma; Ōhiroma of the Ninomaru Palace, Nijō Castle.

and the lintel of the *tokonoma*, which effects a smooth visual transition from the side wall to the back.

Like the staggered shelves, the *tsukeshoin* became increasingly varied in style, many examples incorporating in the back wall a Chinese-influenced ogee-arched window (*katōmado*). A later and simpler version also came into use known as the *hirashoin* ("flat *shoin*"), so called because it included no alcove or writing desk but simply windowlike *shōji* set into the wall. Transom styles multiplied as well. The desk was not, however, originally known as the *tsukeshoin* but rather as the *dashifuzukue* ("desk for putting out writings"). It was also called the *shoin*, probably because it was as a matter of course built into the study room bearing that name. The term *tsukeshoin* came into use only when it became necessary to differentiate between the flat *hirashoin* and the orthodox alcove type. Like the shelves, the *tsukeshoin* could be used as a display area, and was often adorned with costly ink sticks, ink stones, brushes, paperweights, and water jars.

Across from the *tsukeshoin* in the Jōdan no Ma of the Ōhiroma audience hall are the decorative doors, the *chōdaigamae*, composed of four regally-appointed *fusuma* screens set in frames of black lacquer studded with gold fittings (pls. 2, 6). The inner two panels can be slid behind the two fixed outer ones by means of the two heavy orange tassels. The upper sill of these doors is lower than the mid-wall frieze rail, and the lower sill is level with the floor boards of the other three *shoin* fixtures. *Chōdaigamae* literally means "sleeping-room appurtenance," a name descriptive of its original function as the entrance to a sleeping chamber. The *chōdaigamae* of the audience hall, however, reflects a later development in that it does not open on to a sleeping area but rather serves simply as an entrance and egress for the master of the palace (pl. 7). As retainers might be located behind the doors during interviews, the *chōdaigamae* is also sometimes called a *mushakakushi*, or "warrior concealer."

These four interior elements—the *tokonoma*, staggered shelves, *tsukeshoin*, and *chōdaigamae*—all existed in the Muromachi period (1333–1567), but it was not until the Momoyama period (1568–1614) that all four came to be assembled in one room. This is one criterion for a mature *shoin* structure. Furthermore, although all four elements were originally located in private areas of the residence, in the mature *shoin* they have moved to the public area. In fact, these were the elements defining the area of greatest formality; only the highest ranking person present at an audience was allowed to be seated in the space they demarcated. The relationship of these elements, especially the *tokonoma*, to high social rank became, in fact, codified in the Edo period, and people below a certain station were prohibited by law from building them.

The change in location of the four *shoin* fixtures from private study or sleeping areas to public ones accompanied a general shift in emphasis from the private to the public areas of residences. Even today, in the modern traditional-style Japanese house, the best room, which incorporates at least a *tokonoma*, is reserved for the entertainment of guests. It may be that private interviews were originally held in the study area which included some of these fixtures and so gradually came to be associated with an audience function. As the *tokonoma*, staggered shelves, and *tsukeshoin* came to be associated not with study but with audiences, it was natural that their decorative and symbolic functions took precedence over their functional roles. The end result of this is seen in the Jōdan no Ma of the Ōhiroma audience hall, where all four elements are used to signify the place of greatest importance in the building. The staggered shelves and *tsukeshoin* are no longer functionally linked but are placed on opposite sides of the *tokonoma*, with the effect that the central importance of the *tokonoma* is strengthened and a greater sense of balance between it and the lower *tsukeshoin* and staggered shelves is achieved.

The mandatory inclusion of all four elements, or at least a combination of some of them, in the main room of a residence introduced a degree of standardization into the upper-class residential scheme. From an artistic point of view this means that variation in detail is of great importance. Slight differences in detail from building to building

6. *Chōdaigamae* of the Jōdan no Ma; Ōhiroma of the Ninomaru Palace, Nijō Castle.

7. *Chōdaigamae* of the Jōdan no Ma; Ōhiroma of the Ninomaru Palace, Nijō Castle.

are often the product of careful artistic consideration, and full appreciation of the scope of the *shoin* style demands sensitivity to these seemingly minor variations. It is for this reason that the author of this book is at great pains to bring our attention not only to the immediately apparent aspects of the buildings he introduces, but also to small differences in room area and decor.

The Ōhiroma audience hall of the Ninomaru Palace is one of the most splendid and fully realized examples of a standard *shoin* interior, and represents the greatest dimensions the palatial *shoin* was to attain. But it does not reflect the final development of the basic *shoin* plan. Hirai, in his article noted earlier, tells why this is so. In Muromachi times (1333–1567) the main building of most upper-class domestic structures incorporated both public and private areas under one roof, with the private rooms usually at the north. As time progressed, however, the area for formal interviews and various public functions grew in importance and was gradually separated from the private living areas. The main building, now used for only public functions, grew in size in response to the increasing stress on formal audiences, coming to be known as the *hiroma* or "great hall." The main audience area within this hall included not one space but two or three, with different floor levels to emphasize the status distinctions which were observed with increasing rigidity within the military-dominated society of the time. But this *hiroma* (also called *ōhiroma* in some buildings) still contained rooms to the north which had been needed when both public and private spaces were included in the main building. As long as superior and inferior were different, clearly demarcated spaces, interviews could be conducted either in two rooms oriented east and west, or in two rooms arranged north and south. In the case of the Ōhiroma complex of the Ninomaru Palace, there were instances when the shogun would be in the Jōdan no Ma and the *daimyō* lords to the south in the Gedan no Ma, and also instances when the shogun himself would be located in the Gedan no Ma and the lower-placed participants to the east in the San no Ma (pl. 8). This "L" plan is a characteristic of the *hiroma* style.

When the other daimyo built their mansions in Edo in response to the Tokugawa requirement that they "alternate attendance" between their home fiefs and the capital (*sankin kōtai*), they constructed their mansions in the manner of the shogunal palaces, insofar as their finances and Tokugawa sumptuary laws allowed. But after the devastating Meireki fire of 1657, most daimyo rebuilt their mansions on a simplified scale, abandoning the multiple-row plan of the *hiroma* in favor of single-row structures. The Ōhiroma complex of the Ninomaru Palace thus represents the most luxurious and large-scale form of the standard *shoin* style, but not its final development.

At the same time that Hideyoshi's *shoin* structures were setting a new standard in magnificence, the tea ceremony was reaching its mature phase under Hideyoshi's tea master, Sen no Rikyū (1522–91). The teahouses built to accommodate this ceremony incorporated elements from the Japanese farmhouse, and represented a very different

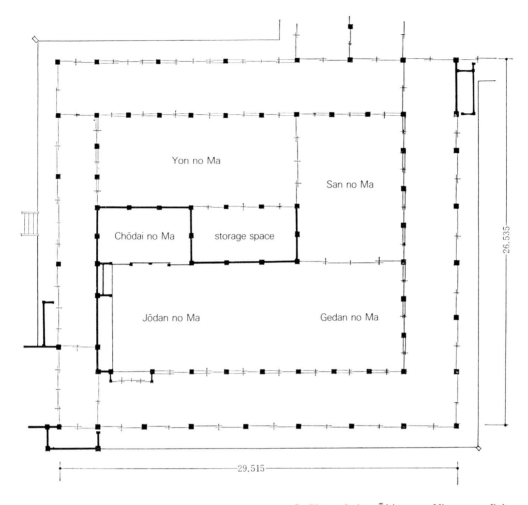

Yon no Ma

San no Ma

Chōdai no Ma

storage space

Jōdan no Ma

Gedan no Ma

26.535

29.515

8. Plan of the Ōhiroma; Ninomaru Palace, Nijō Castle.

set of values from those stressed in the vast audience halls of Hideyoshi and of the military leaders who came after him. Where the builders of the Ninomaru Palace of Iemitsu emphasized dazzling color, spacious size, and costly appointments in order to create an effect of awesome power and inapproachable authority, teahouse designers prized human dimensions, natural materials, and simplicity as backdrops for the realization of values derived from Zen Buddhism and associated with the tea ceremony, such as harmony between man and his natural environment, refinement of taste, elegant restraint, and spiritual repose.

At an early stage, however, the teahouse, known also as a *sukiya,* and the *shoin* sometimes merged, giving rise to the *sukiya shoin,* or, simply, the *sukiya* style for residences. On the other hand, teahouses favored by daimyo lords also were influenced by the *shoin* style. The introduction into the *shoin* scheme of simple and understated teahouse elements produced a more relaxed architecture, well suited to areas for everyday life and informal meetings.

One of the best examples of a building in the *sukiya shoin* style is the Kuroshoin of Nishi Hongan-ji, the head temple of the Jōdo Shinshū sect of Buddhism. Constructed in 1656–57, it served as the private residence of the head priest, and its style is appropriate to this living-area function. The Kuroshoin is connected by a corridor to the north side of the Shiroshoin (pl. 96), mentioned earlier as being, along with the Ninomaru Palace, a fine example of the ornate *shoin* style of the Kan'ei era (1624–44) of the early Edo period. As we have seen, the division of the Kuroshoin living area from the Shiroshoin audience area is characteristic of mature *shoin* structures. Like the Ōhiroma of the Ninomaru Palace, the Kuroshoin is composed of a number of spaces, arranged in two rows with the two most important rooms, the Ichi no Ma and Ni no Ma, situated side by side at the south (pl. 142). These two spaces show the same structural framework as the Ōhiroma of the Ninomaru Palace, but the effect attained is vastly different, demonstrating the great latitude inherent in the *shoin* style.

Whereas the purpose of the Ninomaru Ōhiroma was to provide a place of grandeur for formal audiences, the Ichi no Ma and Ni no Ma of the Kuroshoin were built to serve as an area for the head priest of an extremely influential temple to live and carry out day-to-day business, hold informal interviews, and conduct the tea ceremony in an appended tearoom (pls. 9, 137–38). Its design was thus not meant to awe but to provide a relaxed atmosphere for a man of learning and sophisticated tastes. It is a marvelous gem of a building, constructed with the expert carpenter's painstaking attention to finish and detail. As with a piece of elegant furniture, woods of the best quality have been chosen for the room, and have been finished so as to make their natural beauty come forth most effectively.

Wood is the heart of the *sukiya*, and the best residences show an extraordinary sensitivity to the varied effects different woods provide. In the alcove housing the Katsura Shelves in the New Palace of the Katsura Detached Palace (pls. 10, 151) are found paulownia, persimmon, betal nut, red sandalwood, ebony, chinese quince, bombay blackwood, horse chestnut, zelkova, and mulberry, as well as the more commonly used cryptomeria. The location of each is determined on the basis of its grain, color, and texture. The treatment of wood in the Kuroshoin reveals the basic philosophy of the entire structure, that is, the careful choice and fastidious treatment of materials to suggest at once naiveté and sophistication, naturalness and refinement, art without artfulness. The materials speak for themselves, not relying for their effect on a painted or gilded finish. Except for those in the corners, the posts of the Kuroshoin are not smooth and square-cut like those of the Ninomaru Ōhiroma. Instead, they are somewhat roughly worked, with their original loglike texture retained at the corners. These posts (*menkawa-bashira*) are characteristic of the *sukiya* style, and they introduce a feeling of softness and naturalness into the room. The *fusuma* screens are not of the ornate polychrome and gold type, but have instead been decorated with ink monochrome landscapes, which lend a subdued tone to the interior, the explosion

10. The Katsura Shelves of the New
Palace, Katsura Detached Palace.

of color seen earlier being traded here for tones of grays and black which harmonize with the unfinished wood and emphasize its natural luster. The *kokabe*, finished in gold and polychrome before, are left bare, but rendered in colored ochre rather than in white, this addition of color to the plaster walls being found in many *sukiya* structures. Frequently the plaster finish is quite rough in the *sukiya* style as well. Naturally-finished wood is also used in the ceiling, here hung in a manner often seen in *sukiya* structures, with unpainted planks visually supported by battens (*saobuchi*). Although many *sukiya* structures dispense with frieze rails entirely, they have been retained in the Kuroshoin of the Nishi Hongan-ji, giving it a more formal air than other *sukiya* dwellings. But the frieze rails here are thinner than in the Ninomaru Ōhiroma, in keeping with the smaller dimensions of the Kuroshoin rooms themselves. This is true as well of the posts, and in general there is an air of delicacy and lightness which stands in strong contrast to the oppressive majesty of the sturdy members used at Nijō Castle. The feeling of buoyancy is emphasized by the delicate paintings on the *fusuma* screens, by the thin battens, and by the unpainted finish of the ceiling. In addition, the transom between the Ichi no Ma and the Ni no Ma is composed of a latticework of narrow vertical and horizontal strips interspersed with filigreed motifs, which counters the brittle quality of the verticals and horizontals and yields, overall, a gentle, even whimsical effect typical of the best *sukiya* dwellings.

A fanciful, imaginative rethinking of the formal *shoin* scheme is characteristic of the *sukiya* style. This creativity explains why the *sukiya* style retained its vitality long after many houses built in the standard *shoin* manner had become artistically stagnant. Whereas it became obligatory for the formal *shoin* room to have a *tokonoma* and staggered shelves on the back wall with the *tokonoma* closer to the veranda, a *tsukeshoin* desk on the veranda wall itself and decorative doors (*chōdaigamae*) on the wall opposite, the *sukiya shoin* shows endless variation in the placement of these fixtures.

The Kuroshoin is famous for its interior plan. The *tokonoma* is here located away from the veranda, and beside it is not an alcove with staggered shelves but a *tsukeshoin*, recessed well behind the front of the *tokonoma* (pls. 137–38). The corner with the *tsukeshoin* is illuminated not only from directly behind but also from the transom above and a window in the veranda wall. This comparatively large number of openings combines with the recessed nature of the desk to suggest that, as opposed to the purely decorative function of this fixture in the Ōhiroma audience hall of the Ninomaru Palace, it can actually function here as a study area, the purpose for which the *tsukeshoin* was originally developed. The window decorating the back wall of the desk contains a Chinese-influenced ogee arch, a motif often found in *sukiya* buildings. The materials of which the *tokonoma* is composed are more congenial than those of the Ōhiroma—a soft *tatami* floor and a decorative lacquer molding (*kamachi*) which sits directly on the main *tatami* floor, not being raised above it by a narrow band of wall as was the floorboard of the Ninomaru Palace. The rough post at the corner of the

30

11. Staggered shelves of the Ichi no Ma;
Kuroshoin, Nishi Hongan-ji.

tokonoma (*tokobashira*) and the half-wall (*sodekabe*) behind it are also tea-inspired elements often seen in structures of this sort.

One of the most famous elements of the Kuroshoin, and one which gives a particularly clear idea of *sukiya* taste, is the shelf alcove, placed imaginatively in the veranda wall (pls. 11, 138). This too has the cabinets seen earlier, but the shelves themselves are not the dignified tripartite *seirō-dana* type used often in palatial *shoin* buildings; instead they show an extremely light configuration wherein one middle shelf on the left balances two on the right, all three being reinforced by a central post hung from above (pl. 143). They do not fit into the back wall but rather have individual backings with complicated openwork designs.

The Kuroshoin is also typical of *sukiya* designs in that it has a tearoom (pl. 145), in this case entered through sliding *fusuma* next to the shelves of the Ichi no Ma. It is also representative of the style in that it lacks certain palatial *shoin* elements, most notably the decorative doors (*chōdaigamae*) and the raised-floor section (*jōdan*). In the *sukiya shoin* that do have *jōdan*, these areas usually are arranged to provide an atmosphere for study and relaxation rather than to emphasize hierarchical status.

There can be no question but that the Kuroshoin is as elegant as the Ōhiroma audience hall at the Ninomaru Palace, but the elegance is of a profoundly different

31

character. Here the beauty resides in simplicity and restraint. The materials used in the Kuroshoin rely on their inherent qualities for their beauty—the satiny luster and well-worn grain of the aged wood of the posts and veranda floorboards rather than polychrome designs and gilded metal fixtures. Just as the absence of furniture makes one look more closely at the structure of the building itself, so the avoidance of poly-chrome and gold brings out the qualities of the components themselves. To walk down a veranda at the Kuroshoin or the Katsura Detached Palace is to deepen one's ap-preciation of wood itself, through the eye, the nose, and the soles of one's stocking feet. This architecture impresses upon us more than any other that a building owes its existence in equal parts to the hand of man and to the natural world.

The emphasis in the *sukiya* on natural materials—wooden members, grass mats, mud-and-plaster walls—reflects the integration of traditional Japanese residential architecture with its natural surroundings. This is less obvious at Nishi Hongan-ji, located in the middle of Kyoto, than it is at the Katsura Detached Palace, situated in the southwest suburbs of that city. There the unity of the unfinished wooden posts, the woven rush *tatami*, and the brown roofs with the trees and lawns around them is immediately apparent. In order to reach the main complex at Katsura, one is led down a long path which passes through rustic gates and over an earthen bridge. The walk at once refreshes and calms, and also heightens awareness of the natural surroundings. It modulates the transition from the hectic outside world to one of seclusion and heightened sensitivity. The complex itself looks out over a landscape garden of ponds and hillocks, streams and pathways which can be appreciated from most of the interior rooms due to the staggered plan of the complex, or enjoyed by passing through the gardens on foot or by boat. This is a nobleman's private Xanadu, with priceless rocks placed by artisans who dedicated their lives to choosing and locat-ing them properly, and with shoals and islands designed to recall to a cultured ob-server famous scenic spots mentioned in classical literature. Whereas the Ninomaru Palace was designed for the business of ruling, Katsura, begun at roughly the same time, was arranged to provide for a courtier's relaxation.

The buildings and the gardens of the Katsura complex are positioned in sympathy with each other. From the Moon-viewing Platform of the Old Shoin (pl. 12) one sees, in receding order, the pond, then the tip of the Shinsen islets on which is ar-ranged a still life of pines and rocks around a miniature stone pagoda, then the Shōkin-tei teahouse amidst the taller trees of the background. It is a composition of subtle modulations between the buildings and the garden. These structures have a great calmness. The natural coloration does not reflect and dazzle but rather relaxes and leads to composure of the mind, the accents of more vivid color here and there adding an element of the fanciful. The buildings are silent as well, with few hard surfaces to cause reverberation, and we thus become more attuned to the sound of the wind through the surrounding trees, of a brook, or of a songbird.

The interrelationship between the architecture and nature is not limited to sight

12. Moon-viewing Platform of the Old
Shoin, Katsura Detached Palace.

lines and choice or treatment of building materials. Instead, the structure actually merges into the garden. Plate 13 presents a view of the Old Shoin from the pond. Flat rocks meander asymmetrically up the shallow bank toward the Moon-viewing Platform. Halfway up they intersect with a stone path whose ruler-straight sides are parallel to the veranda. This path, not visible in the picture, prepares one who has just alighted from a boat at the pond's edge for entry into the Old Shoin. Directly in front of the low plaster wall of the building is a stone step on which footgear is left. The "shoe-removing stone" (*kutsu-nugi ishi*) bridges the difference in height between the ground and the veranda. One then progresses to a wooden step, whose height and material continue the visual as well as the physical modulatory process; then to the veranda itself, an element which, we are told by Ōta Hirotarō, "seems part of the outdoors when seen from the inside, but . . . looks like part of the house when seen from the garden."[8] In the two buildings to the left in plate 13, the verandas are now enclosed with sliding screens, but the Old Shoin retains an older design in which the veranda is left open to the weather, facilitating an effective transition between the outside and the living space. Because it is summer, the screens on the inside periphery of the veranda have been removed, further emphasizing the interrelationship between inside and out. The plaster wall beneath the outer lip of the veranda and the *kokabe* of the interior are of identical material, and the same posts relate to both the interior and exterior spaces. The total result is a perfectly realized modulation of interior and exterior space. This leads the viewer to appreciate the essential oneness of the world outside with the architecture and himself. The building serves as the intermediary between its makers and that of which it is made, allowing man to be protected from the elements while being in intimate contact with them. Man does not attempt to conquer nature here as he often does in the West, but rather works toward harmony with nature.

But simplicity and naturalness are not enough to make a structure artistically worthwhile. What makes Katsura and the Kuroshoin works of art is the refinement with which the simple elements have been utilized. They are products of the same precise craftsmanship that yielded the more immediately electrifying Tokugawa palaces. The choice of materials, colors, and textures, and the manner in which they are finished and arranged show great sophistication. Everything unites to yield a design that is both natural and elegant, fanciful yet dignified. The simplicity of the conception demands for its success perfection in its execution—a minor misstep in the location of a post or in the choice or finish of the various woods is magnified in this architecture and destroys the delicate balance of the room as a whole. A gnarled post may be irregularly shaped, but to be effective in a *sukiya* scheme its irregularity must be exactly right for the space itself—it must be perfect in its imperfection. The same is true of the garden. Each stone and tree has been chosen for its particular quality and located for maximum effect. Both the building and the garden stress naturalness, but it is a minutely planned nature.

13. View from the pond of the main complex of
Katsura Detached Palace.

Even though we have stressed the differences between the splendid Ōhiroma of the Ninomaru Palace and the more restrained Kuroshoin and Katsura villa, it must be added that the whole Nijō Castle complex is related more closely to the other two buildings than a comparison of isolated elements suggests. There is a fine garden area at Nijō too (pl. 91); furthermore, the constituent buildings are laid out on the same staggered plan as at Katsura, and for the same reason—to increase the number of rooms with direct lighting and good views of the natural surroundings. At the same time, the private living quarters of the master of the palace at Nijō, the Shiroshoin, are much closer in feeling to the Kuroshoin of Nishi Hongan-ji than is the Ōhiroma.

The basic reason why all three structures, roughly contemporary in date, are masterpieces of the *shoin* style is that their contrasting moods have been created by differing treatments of essentially the same basic architectural program. This *shoin* style is based on the post and lintel system, with nonbearing walls or screens between the uprights. Straight line predominates in elevation as in plan and contributes a steady rhythm to interiors through repetition of the post element. The distance between posts is known as a *ken* (bay) and is the same throughout a room and indeed throughout most of the structure, though exceptions do exist. The *ken* is a module which allows the asymmetrical and nonaxial plans of the Ninomaru Palace and Katsura to retain an inner order. Interior space is subdivided by *fusuma* sliding screens, usually two per bay, or by fixed walls of bamboo laths with clay-and-straw fill and plaster finish. Exterior walls are often composed of sliding elements. In the older *shoin* dwellings, two sliding wooden doors (*mairado*) are combined with one *shōji* sliding screen behind. On later buildings is seen an unbroken row of wainscoted *shōji* guarded from the rain when necessary by removable rain doors (*amado*). Both interior and exterior screens can be either totally closed, or slid open one behind the other, or removed entirely, providing a great number of possible variations in the lighting and ventilation of the interior. The illustration of the Old Shoin at Katsura (pl. 13) shows the appearance of a room with the exterior screens removed. It is at once apparent how well suited the style is for summer weather. The flexibility of inner partitioning allows for the creation of small, totally enclosed spaces or great open ones within the same structure, depending on the needs of the moment. The relative lack of furniture adds to the feeling of great openness encountered in the *shoin* style. Above the screens, however, are frieze rails and fixed walls (*kokabe*), which define space even when the screens themselves are slid back or removed.

The post and lintel system with screen walls also makes this architecture very two-dimensional and results in a lack of building-surface plasticity. This characteristic, however, contributes much to the overall sense of geometry inherent in these spaces. The order and harmony of the room and of the whole structure is further insured through the use of *kiwari*, the system for interrelating the size, proportion, and placement of all constituent parts of a building, according to pre-established measurements. Furthermore, as Ōta Hirotarō points out, "The distance between two adjacent columns is a fixed unit. There are two systems of measuring these units: the *kyōma* (Kyoto system) and the *inakama* (provincial system). All measurements in the building plan are multiples of the half unit."[9]

The floors of the *shoin* are in general covered with straw mats (*tatami*) which vary in dimension from one part of the country to another, but are roughly one meter by two meters in size. This approximates the size of one person's sleeping mattress, thus strengthening the relationship between man and his living space. As will be seen in the text, room sizes are reckoned not in meters but in the number of mats inside. The floor plan of a *shoin* building is thus composed of squares and rectangles, which has led many to remark on the similarity of this architecture and the designs of Mondrian.

The plan of a typical *shoin* complex includes several structures, divided according to the function each is to play. It is arranged asymmetrically and without a clear axial progression from major spaces to minor ones, this in contrast to many European styles. Arthur Drexler comments that "Space in Japanese architecture is additive. . . . In the view which regards architecture as a kind of music, Japanese architecture is a thoughtful meandering along a keyboard."[10] As we have seen, however, the architecture relates with great precision to its natural surroundings in terms of vistas, and constituent rooms and buildings are in harmony with each other because of the same modular design system used for all the parts. True, variations in bay dimension do occasionally occur from room to room, or even within the same room, as in the Audience Hall of the Nishi Hongan-ji, where the two bays closest to the far wall are shorter than the others in the room to give the illusion of greater depth. In general, however, the bay dimension remains constant. The importance of a space is expressed more through its size and appointments than by its position, though certain conventions of placement according to function are seen. Two other features normally required by the *shoin* scheme are verandas around the main buildings and, by the Edo period, entryways (*genkan*).

To this basic structural basis are added the elements we have previously discussed, such as the *tokonoma*, staggered shelves, *tsukeshoin*, and decorative doors (*chōdaigamae*), the raised-floor areas (*jōdan*), transom, frieze rails, and either coffered or battened ceilings, according to the function the structure was to carry out. The *shoin* style thus incorporates a distinct set of general rules to be followed and elements to be included, but allows great variation within these guidelines in order to suit a great variety of needs. Like the traditional Japanese thirty-one syllable *waka* poem, which must be broken into fixed lines of 5, 7, 5, 7, and 7 syllables each, the basic rules of the *shoin* are to a great extent preordained—the art is seen in the way variations are introduced into the basic framework and in the level of refinement with which the basic elements are treated. To appreciate the variations, one must have a familiarity with the *shoin* themes. That is what the author of this book, through the introduction of the best extant *shoin* examples, attempts to provide.

While it is hoped that this work will lead to a satisfying appreciation of the *shoin* style, no publication can match the experience of visiting the sites in person. The author has accordingly chosen for his study only extant *shoin* structures that can be enjoyed by readers fortunate enough to spend time in Japan. These are arranged chronologically, with *sukiya shoin* as well as *minka shoin* (commoners' homes that incorporate *shoin* elements) given separate chapters. All are provided with floor plans as well as addresses in an appendix.

As the author wrote the original work for a Japanese audience, he assumed a general familiarity with the history and culture of the country. I have therefore added background information on the times in which the buildings were constructed, on the major personages that figured in the building histories, and on basic artistic currents that came into play in the design process. All errors in the final text are my responsibility.

A great debt of thanks is owed Dr. John Rosenfield of Harvard University for his editorial guidance and constant encouragement throughout the translation process. I am also indebted to Dr. Hirai Kiyoshi of the Tokyo Institute of Technology, Mr. Charles Terry, and Dr. Mary Parent for numerous helpful suggestions on the manuscript, and to Mr. Michael Brase of Kodansha International.

H. Mack Horton

1

ORIGIN OF THE SHOIN STYLE

The word *shoin* has undergone a complex evolution, its meaning varying according to historical period. Originally, the *shoin* referred to a single room used for study and daily living. In Zen temples in particular, the corner room of the abbot's quarters (*hōjō*) reserved for these functions is often known as the *shoin*. In this room came to be incorporated, singly or in combination, several prescribed architectural elements. These were the *tsukeshoin*, a low, broad wooden surface for reading and writing with window illumination, the *chigaidana*, built-in staggered shelves, and the *tokonoma*, an alcove for the display of art objects such as hanging scrolls, ceramics, or flower arrangements. These elements gradually came to be incorporated into the main room of a structure, the entire building taking on the name *shoin*. At its most advanced stage, the *shoin* style describes a complex of buildings of varying character, one or more rooms incorporating the above elements. Complete understanding of the *shoin* style requires consideration of the surviving examples of each of these stages of development, be they early *shoin* structures such as the Tōgu-dō of Ginkaku-ji or mature *choin* complexes exemplified by the Ninomaru Palace of Nijō Castle.

The main predecessor of the *shoin* style is the *shinden*, a mode of building which reached maturity in the Heian period (782–1184), the classical era of Japan's cultural history when native modes of expression in calligraphy, poetry, and painting were also developed. Architectural historians have traditionally designated two intermediary residential styles from the course of *shinden* to *shoin* development. These are the *shuden* style, for which the Kōjō-in Guest Hall is often given as a prime example, and the *buke* (warrior house) style, variously classed as the precursor of the *shuden* or a synonym for it. Modern research has, however, shown these intermediate styles to reproduce earlier ideas or prefigure the *shoin* type, and it is now considered more accurate to deal with them not as distinct and independent building styles but, in general, as either variations on the *shinden* type or as early forms of the *shoin*. Discussion of the *shoin* style thus becomes broader and more complex by the inclusion of these hitherto separate types.

The influence the *shoin* style exerted was, in turn, as varied and broad as its path of development. Perfected in the sixteenth and seventeenth centuries as the residential

39

style of the warrior class, it was quickly adopted by the clergy for temple residences. More wide reaching, however, was its effect on the residences of all the upper classes. It was incorporated into many of the building schemes of aristocrats who had hitherto favored the classic *shinden* style. *Shoin* elements, too, found their way into the main room and guest rooms of the official residences of town administrators and wealthy merchants. From this point the style was gradually absorbed into the dwellings of the common people, and even today it is fundamental to Japan's domestic architecture.

The intrinsic beauty of *shoin* buildings is of course a primary reason why a style born of a feudal era has enjoyed such popularity and longevity. Another factor in its success, though, is the inherent flexibility and variety of its constituent parts, a quality which recommended it to members of many different classes and tastes. On the one hand the mature *shoin* style provided an opulent and majestic style well suited to the residences of daimyo lords and to large temple compounds, amply reflecting the awe-inspiring formality inherent to warrior society in the Momoyama and Edo periods. Yet as the style developed, it incorporated as well the gentler, more mellow aspects of the teahouse. This *sukiya shoin* was gradually simplified and became genial and approachable. In this form it diffused into the lower classes and came into widespread use.

THE SHINDEN STYLE

The *shoin* reached its mature form in the first half of the seventeenth century, that form consisting of several independent buildings formed into a unified residential space. The style had, however, been gradually taking shape throughout Japan's medieval period (1185–1567). As noted above, it developed in general from the *shinden* residence favored by the upper class in the Heian period (782–1184), and its evolution cannot be fully appreciated without a general understanding of its *shinden* predecessors.

The most prominent extant example of the *shinden* type is the Kyoto Imperial Palace, which is a reconstruction of far older forms. But the essential elements of the basic *shinden* plan can perhaps be best understood by early representations found in narrative picture scrolls (*emakimono*) and descriptions in old diaries. A particularly noteworthy account of the ideal *shinden* residence can be found in the *Kaoku zakkō*, a treatise on architecture by Sawada Natari (1775–1845). In this illustration (pl. 14) the central hall (the *shinden*, from which the style as a whole takes its name) is flanked to the east and west by outlying structures called *tai-no-ya*. They are connected to the central *shinden* by roofed corridors known as *rō*. The *rō* extend south from both *tai-no-ya* as well to connect two small kiosklike structures, the one to the east here labeled the *izumi-dono* ("fountain pavilion") and that to the west the *tsuri-dono* ("fishing pavilion"). Because the *rō* passageways leading to these pavilions are bisected by "middle gates" (*chūmon*) they are also known as *chūmon-rō*. The complex opens to the south, the court-

14. A *shinden* complex (from *Kaoku zakkō*).

15. A *shinden* complex (model of the Hōjū-
ji villa, Kanagawa Prefectural Museum).

yard being landscaped with a pond and formal garden. Modified left-right symmetry is a predominant characteristic of this ideal plan. The symmetry, southern orientation, and building-garden relationship reflect Chinese ideas, the fashions from the continent having great influence on the formation of Japanese concepts.

The interior elements of the *shinden* style can likewise be gleaned from early literary sources. They show it to have possessed a marked fluidity of arrangement in room division and function. Space partitioning was effected to some degree by fixed walls but more often by blinds (*sudare*) of woven rush or bamboo strips, movable curtain stands (*kichō*), and other devices, all of which could be easily opened or removed. The scarcity of actual walls made privacy as Westerners know it almost unobtainable in the *shinden* dwelling. Floors were of wood, with portable straw mats being laid down individually where necessary. Furniture was rarely used, and that which was, such as the *dashifu-zukue* desk and the movable shelves mentioned in the Introduction, was portable. Interiors were thus sparse, and easily rearranged. A hint of the atmosphere inside the *shinden* can be gathered from the description of an evening scene given by Sei Shōnagon in her famous mid-Heian *Pillow Book* (*Makura no sōshi*):

> The floor-boards in the ante-room are shining so brightly that they mirror everything near by, and some crisp new straw matting has been placed near the three-foot curtain of state. The curtains themselves give a lovely cool impression. . . .
>
> By the light of the lamp one can see that the blinds further back in the room have been raised all the way; below them several women . . . sit leaning against the raised beam between the ante-room and the veranda. In another part of the room some more ladies are huddled together under a closed blind. A fire is smouldering deep in the incense-burner, giving out a scent that is vaguely melancholy and full of calm elegance.[11]

The interface between interior and exterior was to a large degree variable as well. The interior could be opened to the outside when so desired by swinging up the top halves of the heavy reticulated shutters (*shitomido*) and fixing them to the overhanging eaves by means of long, suspended hooks. The bottom halves could be then lifted out and the *sudare* blinds either left in place or rolled up to effect a complete spatial continuum from interior to veranda to garden, putting the house in intimate touch with the natural world. The columns between the reticulated shutters were round; it was not until sliding doors came to be commonly used on exteriors that the square posts of the *shoin* came to be employed.

Natural hues predominate in the *shinden*, with bark-shingled roofs and walls of unpainted wood and white plaster. Due to the long eave overhang, these interiors were more often than not quite dark, and their depressing effect in poor weather is often bemoaned in the literature of the time. The gloom was mitigated somewhat, however, by touches of color, on the silk borders of the blinds and *tatami*, on the screens and curtains, and of course in the garments of the inhabitants themselves. Again, Sei Shōnagon's contemporary comment: "Bright green bamboo blinds are a delight, especially when beneath them one can make out the many layers of a woman's clothes emerging from under brilliantly colored curtains of state."[12]

LATER DEVELOPMENT OF THE SHINDEN

Although bilateral symmetry with the *shinden* hall at the center was apparently considered the ideal configuration, it seems almost never to have been fully attained in actual structures. Furthermore, as time progressed more and more marked asymmetry developed in response to changes in the structure and in the function of the interior space. In the early stages of *shinden* design, the spacious main hall was used for a variety of purposes. As time passed, however, the areas for formal and public use came to be more strictly differentiated from those used when informality and privacy were desired. The central space (*moya*) under the main roof of the *shinden* hall came to be reserved for the more ceremonial functions, with the subordinate spaces (*hisashi*) which surrounded the *moya* being used for day-to-day living. As time progressed, the *hisashi* were augmented, especially at the north, by tertiary spaces called *mago-bisashi*. Thus the gradual functional differentiation between public and private spaces led to a greater compartmentalization of the *shinden* space and necessitated more definite interior partitioning.

GENESIS OF THE SHOIN STYLE

Gradually, then, the interior of the central hall of the *shinden* complex underwent changes in use and configuration. As the outer spaces (the *hisashi* and *mago-bisashi*) developed, partitions were more frequently included and column placement arranged in a less regular way. The division between public and private spaces became more marked, and an area specifically for the reception of guests, called the *kaisho*, was introduced. These new architectural elements were related to, among other factors, changes in patterns of daily living accompanying the rise of the warrior class. Moreover, as will be discussed in greater detail further on, because a major element of military life was the Zen sect, the plan and interior configuration of warrior homes were influenced by those of the abbot's quarters and the kitchens of Zen temples. In sum, then, the process of evolution from the *shinden* to the *shoin* style took place against major changes in social conditions, from the domination of the aristocracy to the rule of the warrior class, with developments in life style bringing about advances in domestic architecture.

43

2

THE EARLY SHOIN STYLE

The relationship between the military rulers of Japan and the Zen creed was, as mentioned above, a far-ranging one. It was the military class, in particular the Kamakura shogunate, which provided the first support for the new Zen sect introduced from China in the late twelfth and early thirteenth centuries by the monks Eisai (1141–1215) and Dōgen (1200–1253). Zen monks served the shogunate not only as spiritual advisors but as authorities on China in general, as many had spent considerable time in training in that country and mastered the Chinese language in order to read the basic Zen doctrines which had all been formulated in Chinese. With the Japanese court and hereditary aristocracy still dominated by the Esoteric and Pure Land Buddhist sects, it was perhaps natural for the newly introduced Zen teachings to find initial favor with the military authorities lately risen to power. Zen doctrines supplied the shogunate with a less scholastic, more intuitive path to salvation; they stressed personal self-discipline, and greatly appealed to the warrior character. Furthermore, Zen monks advised the military leaders on Chinese artistic and architectural concepts and thus played a central role in furnishing the military with an avenue toward cultural prestige, a commodity hitherto the sole property of the court aristocracy. By virtue of their linguistic abilities, keen minds, and overseas experience, the Zen monks also provided leadership for the Japan-China trade, an important element of the shogunate's financial base.

Given the close relationship between Zen monasteries and the military, it is understandable that elements of Zen architecture, themselves designed in the Chinese *karayō* style to be discussed later, should have influenced the domestic and administrative buildings of the ruling class. And since the residential halls in Zen monasteries incorporated elements of what was to become the *shoin* style, it is here that the search for the origins of the building type which became the mainstay of the warrior class must begin.

Unhappily there remains no single structure from this early period in which all the *shoin* elements appear. Several abbot's quarters remaining from the Muromachi period (1333–1567), however, do provide a basic conception of the nature of this type of structure.

ABBOT'S QUARTERS

The Japanese term for abbot's quarters, *hōjō*, literally means "one *jō* [*tatami*] square" and is taken from the name of the celebrated "ten-foot-square hut" of the legendary Indian Buddhist sage Vimalakīrti, who was especially favored by the Zen sect. Vimalakīrti is said to have miraculously enlarged his small dwelling when a vast number of divine beings wished to visit him, the implication being that a modest structure could encompass all wisdom as embodied in a single wise man. The *hōjō* of a Zen monastery functions as the living quarters and reception area for the abbot, the most spiritually elevated personage in the monastery, and is, of course, much larger than its legendary namesake. The oldest extant *hōjō* is that of the Ryōgin-an (alternately the Ryūgin-an) in Kyoto (pl. 16). It is a subtemple of the great Zen monastery Tōfuku-ji, and is located in the northern part of the temple compound.

The builder of the original Ryōgin-an Hōjō was Mukan Fumon (1212–91), the third abbot of Tōfuku-ji and later the founder of Nanzen-ji. Records indicate that Mukan Fumon's *hōjō* was rebuilt in 1387 and possibly again after that date. It is nearly certain, however, that the building was constructed no later than the early fifteenth century. The plan of the Ryōgin-an Hōjō consists of two rows of three rooms each, a feature shared by the two next-oldest surviving abbot's quarters, at the Ryōgen-in (pl. 18) and at the Daisen-in, two subtemples of Daitoku-ji (pls. 17, 19–20). Both structures bear the name *hondō* (main hall), though they function as *hōjō*, or abbot's quarters. Both were rebuilt following their original configurations in the eighteenth century and are of the two-row, six-room arrangement.

It is true that the interior elements later to become basic to the *shoin*—the *tokonoma*, staggered shelves, *tsukeshoin*, and *chōdaigamae* (decorated doors)—are not found in these buildings. They do, however, have a *genkan*, a formal entryway found in nearly all formal *shoin* residences in the Edo period. Furthermore, while the Ryōgin-an Hōjō still uses *shinden*-style reticulated shutters (*shitomido*) on parts of its exterior, the Daisen-in and Ryōgen-in *hōjō* use *mairado* (sliding wooden doors with applied horizontal strips), which again are characteristic of later non-*shinden* architecture. In all three structures interior space is subdivided—not left open as in *shinden* structures—and interior sliding partitions (*fusuma*) and exterior *shōji* screens are used, as well as square posts. Most importantly, they incorporate quiet rear rooms called *shoin* to which the abbot could retire for reading and relaxation. It was out of this *shoin* study room that the style as a whole developed. Thus the Muromachi Zen residence demonstrates the close relationship between Zen temple styles and the origins of the *shoin*.

Hōjō also often have an adjacent small garden area for the private use of the abbot and his associates. As opposed to the *shinden* garden, which one enjoyed as often as not by boating across its large pond area, these Zen gardens are designed to be ap-

45

16. South facade of the Ryōgin-an Abbot's
Quarters, Tōfuku-ji.

preciated by a stationary viewer. The pond, islands, bridges, waterfalls, and abundant
vegetation of the *shinden* garden give way in monasteries to a more restricted, often
symbolic type of garden. At the Daisen-in, for example, water is represented by white
gravel and mountains or waterfalls by massive stones (pl. 21). The whole natural
world is distilled into a monastery corner and serves not so much for pleasure, as
shinden gardens did, but as a route to refinement of the spirit. Later Zen gardens move
even further away from representing nature, and approach the point of abstract
design. The landscaping of later *shoin* structures bears a great debt to these gardens
46   of the abbot's quarters.

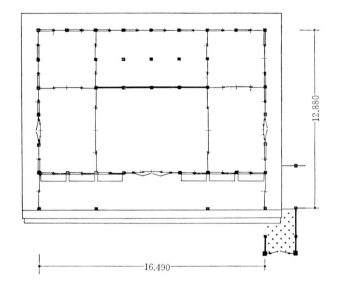

17. Plan of the Ryōgin-an Abbot's Quarters, Tōfuku-ji.

18. South facade of the Ryōgen-in Hondō, Daitoku-ji.

19. Plan of the Ryōgen-in Hondō, Daitoku-ji.

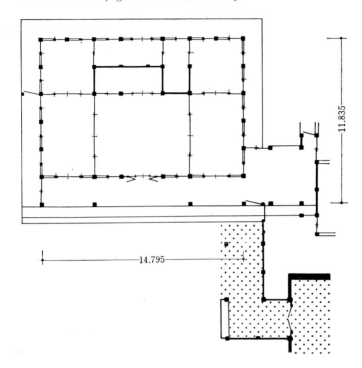

20. Plan of the Daisen-in Hondō, Daitoku-ji.

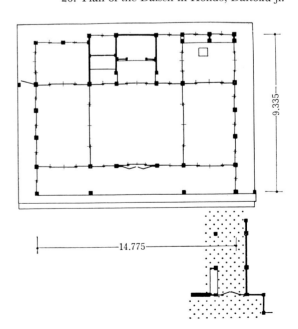

21. Garden of the Daisen-in, Daitoku-ji.

Mansions of the Ashikaga Shogunate

The great mansions built by the leaders of the military government in the Muromachi period (1333–1567) provide another useful view of the transition from the *shinden* to the *shoin* styles of building. The best extant examples are two detached villas, the Kitayama Villa of the third Ashikaga shogun, Yoshimitsu (1358–1408), and the Higashiyama Villa of the eighth Ashikaga shogun, Yoshimasa (1435–90).

The Kitayama Villa and Kinkaku-ji

Of the Kitayama Villa complex only one building remains, the well-known Kinkaku (Golden Pavilion; pl. 22). Though the precinct became the Rokuon-ji temple after Yoshimitsu's death, it is popularly known as the Kinkaku-ji (Temple of the Golden Pavilion). This pavilion, built in 1398 and originally called the Shari-den (Relic Hall), is a *rōkaku*-type structure, a multistory building with close relation to a surrounding landscape garden. Although destroyed by arson on July 2, 1950, it was rebuilt by September of 1955, the reconstruction nearly exactly matching the original through the careful use of old plans and photographs.

The Kitayama complex, built partly as Yoshimitsu's villa and partly as his Zen monastic retreat, was constructed on the site of a thirteenth-century temple, and the existing pond and temple halls were incorporated into the new design. This design was modeled after that of Saihō-ji, one of the masterpieces of the great Zen prelate Musō Soseki (1275–1351). Saihō-ji was originally a Pure Land temple with its own pond and garden related to the *shinden* style of building. In 1339 it was turned over to Musō, who converted it into a Zen monastery and revolutionized garden art. The garden was built in two sections, the northern a dry landscape garden, and the southern a spacious original garden and pond to which Musō added Chinese elements. There he built the two-story Ruri-den (Lapis Lazuli Pavilion), no longer extant, the design of which was based on the *karayō* or "Chinese style" brought from Sung China. The *karayō* style was widely used in Zen structures, and represented a new infusion of Chinese artistic ideas in Japan. Thereafter it coexisted with the older *wayō* ("Japanese style") architecture, which was actually based on Chinese designs imported during the first wave of continental influence in about the T'ang dynasty but had come to be thought of as indigenous by the Kamakura period. The *karayō* is characterized in part by elaborate brackets with carved nosing, located not only above the columns but in the intercolumnar spaces as well. *Karayō* roofs have fan raftering on the corners whereas *wayō* rafters are parallel. Most obviously, the *karayō* style favors the ogee-arched windows (*katōmado*) and paneled Chinese-style doors (*sankarado*).

The Kinkaku-ji garden is basically of the *shinden*-style design, incorporating Zen influences from Saihō-ji. The pond, known as Kyōko (Mirror Lake), is expansive and incorporates many small islands landscaped with pines, shrubs, and majestic rocks. Overlooking this gracious setting is the Golden Pavilion, the counterpart of the Saihō-

22. Kinkaku (Golden Pavilion) viewed from the south; Rokuon-ji.

ji Ruri-den. Covered almost completely with gold leaf, it suggests the splendor and ostentation of Yoshimitsu's taste. The posts of the second floor are thinner than those of the first and those of the third are thinner still, giving a sense of lightness to the structure. The first floor employs *shinden*-style reticulated shutters (*shitomido*) as does part of the second. But the vertical character of the three-story structure is a departure from Heian styles, showing the influence instead of Zen multistory structures such as *sammon* gates and some abbot's quarters and main halls. The third floor is done partially in the *karayō* fashion, with ogee-arched windows and paneled Chinese-style doors (pl. 23). The second floor too, though less conspicuously advanced in style, does include, along with the older *shinden*-style reticulated shutters (*shitomido*), a number of sliding wooden doors (*mairado*). The mingling of elements of the recently imported *karayō* with older *shinden* forms in a private dwelling built by a samurai ruler underscores again the close relationship between the military government and the Zen monasteries where *karayō* forms first appeared in Japan.

51

23. Third floor of the Kinkaku (Golden Pavilion), Rokuon-ji.

The Higashiyama Villa and Ginkaku-ji

The Higashiyama Villa was begun in 1482 by the eighth Ashikaga shogun, Yoshimasa, and building on it continued until his death in 1490. Yoshimasa patterned his villa on the garden and architecture of Saihō-ji as Yoshimasa had, and in 1483 began building a two-story pavilion like the Ruri-den (pl. 24). Housing a votive chapel in the top story, it was named the Kannon-den, and Yoshimasa may have planned to cover it with silver. There is no evidence, however, that the leaf was ever applied, and the Kannon-den, or Ginkaku (Silver Pavilion) as it is popularly known, remains today of natural wood finish. Yoshimasa had large numbers of trees brought in from existing gardens and appropriated some of the rocks in the garden of Kinkaku-ji.

Other buildings in the Higashiyama Villa complex included a *tsune-goten* (private living quarters), *kaisho* (audience hall), and the Tōgu-dō (study and worship hall) to be discussed in the following chapter. According to Yoshimasa's wishes the manor was converted to a temple after his death, and bears the name Jishō-ji. Although the main residential buildings in Yoshimasa's estate no longer remain, we are reminded of its former magnificence by the Silver Pavilion and the Tōgu-dō. Over the years many alterations have been carried out, however, and the garden considerably changed.

As in the case with the Kitayama Villa, the Higashiyama complex occupies a

24. East facade of the Ginkaku (Silver Pavilion), Jishō-ji.

middle step in the transition from the *shinden* to the *shoin* style. Yoshimasa, like his ancestor, had begun to build a *shinden* in his estate just before he died. The Ginkaku, however, shows the influence of post-*shinden* ideas. The first floor uses sliding wooden doors (*mairado*) rather than the reticulated shutters (*shitomido*) of the *shinden* style. Zen influence is again seen in the Chinese-style windows of the second floor, and in elements of the eave bracketing.

It is, however, in the other remaining building of the Higashiyama Villa, the Tōgu-dō, that the departure from the Heian style is most clearly evident. Its northeast room, the Dōjin-sai, provides the earliest surviving example of a *shoin*-style interior.

THE TŌGU-DŌ OF JISHŌ-JI (GINKAKU-JI)

The mansions of both Yoshimitsu and Yoshimasa took their names from their locations in Kyoto—the Kitayama Villa named after the Northern Hills and the Higashiyama Villa after those that rise up to the east. It was to these hills that both men retired after abdicating the office of shogun in favor of their sons. Particularly in Yoshimasa's case, the move away from the official shogunal palace in the Muromachi district of the city provided him with the relative tranquility to engage in his cultural pursuits in the company of many of the finest creative minds in Muromachi Japan. While the capital city itself suffered administrative neglect and incessant political upheaval in the wake of the devastating Ōnin war of 1467 to 1477, Yoshimasa and his coterie gathered in the eastern hills to form an artistic world of surpassing richness. Whereas the Mina-moto and Hōjō clans had operated their military government from Kamakura, weeks away from Kyoto, the Ashikaga had chosen to rule directly from the ancient capital. Yoshimitsu, and Yoshimasa after him, were thus in close touch with the cultural developments within the aristocracy, the military, and the Kyoto Gozan (Five Mon-asteries) of the Zen sect. The artistic style and philosophy which had seen considerable development under Yoshimitsu was a fusion of these strains. In Yoshimasa's era it achieved its apex. Connoisseurship of Chinese paintings and ceramics reached a high level under the eye of artist and aesthetician Nōami (1397–1471) and his descendants. Murata Jukō (1422–1502) began the steps toward the establishment of the tea cere-mony (see Chapter Five), and the Nō drama was adopted as the official entertainment of the shogun. The era which saw this phenomenal artistic development is known as the Higashiyama period, named after the Higashiyama Villa of Yoshimasa which formed its chief focus. Still remaining on the villa site is the building in which the shogun on occasion examined paintings and porcelains with friends, meditated in solitude, and perhaps prepared tea. Known as the Tōgu-dō, it gives along with the Ginkaku an impression of the Higashiyama Villa complex, and provides the earliest glimpse of a *shoin*-style interior.

The Shoin no Ma

The Tōgu-dō (alternately Tōgū-dō) originally served as a *jitsubutsu-dō*, a hall of private worship, for Yoshimasa (pl. 25). The name, literally "Hall of the Eastern Quest," implies living in the east but seeking salvation in the west. It relates to the Sairai-dō (Hall of the Western Arrival) of the Saihō-ji. The Butsuma (Devotional Chamber) of the hall housed a statue of Amida Nyorai, an arrangement which, together with the name of the hall, recalls the fact that while Higashiyama culture owed a great debt to Zen influence, Yoshimasa himself was of the Pure Land faith which promised rebirth in the Western Paradise through supplication to the Buddha Amida. The Tōgu-dō was then not a residential building, but one of its rooms, the Dōjin-sai (Cham-ber of Universal Benevolence), incorporates several elements of crucial importance to the history of Japanese residential architecture (pl. 26). A room of four and a half mats, it includes a shelf alcove a half bay in width, and a one-bay-wide *tsukeshoin* on the north wall (pl. 29). While lacking a *chōdaigamae* and *tokonoma*, it is the oldest extant structure incorporating staggered shelves and *tsukeshoin* alcove. It is a fine example of the early phase of the *shoin* style.

Although the Tōgu-dō was altered several times in succeeding centuries, a full-scale renovation of the building from January 1964 to June 1965 restored it as closely as possible to its original configuration. The plan includes the Butsuma and a four-mat room on the south, the entrance side (pl. 27). At the north are the Dōjin-sai and a six-mat room. The Tōgu-dō resembles in many respects the configuration of the *hōjō* of a Zen monastery, and has a similar wood-floored altar room. The other three

25. South facade of the Tōgu-dō, Jishō-ji.

rooms are floored completely with *tatami* mats and use *fusuma* sliding screens. Sliding wooden doors (*mairado*) in front of *shōji* (sliding screens made of light wooden frames with white paper pasted on one side) are employed on the exterior. The main entrance is fit with paneled Chinese-style doors (*sankarado*), popular in Zen buildings. The Tōgu-dō thus recalls, along with the Ginkaku and the garden, the close relation between structures made for the warrior class and Zen temple architecture.

The Tōgu-dō and the Shoin Style

Although necessitating some recapitulation, it is worthwhile to present in greater detail at this point the elements of the Tōgu-dō which show the *shoin* style. All the rooms other than the Butsuma are relatively small, are floored completely in *tatami*, and are partitioned by *fusuma* sliding screens. This configuration is in marked contrast to the *shinden* style, in which, it will be recalled, *tatami* were used as movable individual seats, the rooms were large, and built-in partitions few. The exterior walls, again, are composed of sliding wooden doors (*mairado*) and *shōji* sliding screens, as opposed to the

55

26. Dōjin-sai viewed from the Rokujō no Ma; Tōgu-dō, Jishō-ji.

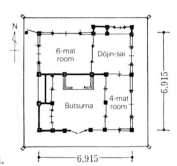

27. Plan of the Tōgu-dō, Jishō-ji.

reticulated shutters (*shitomido*) of *shinden* buildings. In what is perhaps its single most *shoin*-like aspect, the Dōjin-sai has staggered shelves and a *tsukeshoin* alcove set side by side into its north wall (pl. 29). This side-by-side arrangement presents a functional, studious impression, with the shelves seeming a place for putting books and scrolls, and the adjacent *tsukeshoin*, a place for reading them. The simplicity of the *shoin* appointments and the high and thick floorboards of the shelf alcove and *tsukeshoin*, both identical heights above the *tatami*, should be kept in mind as well for comparative purposes further on. It will be recalled from the Introduction, however, that despite this functional arrangement of shelves and *tsukeshoin*, records exist showing that Yoshimasa was well aware of the purely decorative possibilities inherent in these *shoin* elements and exploited them accordingly. The importance of the staggered shelves and *tsukeshoin* cannot be overstated, as these elements are standard in later *shoin* structures.

Another basic element of the *shoin* style, the *tokonoma*, is found in the Tōgu-dō as well. It is, however, in a nascent stage here, being set not into the Dōjin-sai, but rather into the exterior west wall of the Tōgu-dō (pl. 28). Referred to here as the *tokoma*, it has a seat or bench-type character. The shallow depth and marked height of its floor-

28. *"Tokoma"* of the Tōgu-dō, Jishō-ji.

board above the veranda floor level as well reflects its early date. Despite being on the exterior of the structure, the location of the *tokonoma* prefigures that of later buildings in that it is situated where the connecting corridor meets the building proper. Later *tokonoma*, while used as interior—not exterior—features, are still often built into the far wall of the room adjoining the *genkan*, thus retaining the early relationship with the entryway. Despite the careful renovation work, there is still some doubt as to whether the present orientation of the Tōgu-dō is the original. But the present disposition of the connecting corridor leading to it seems to reflect the old plans.

Three of the main interior elements of the *shoin* style are thus in evidence here, establishing the Tōgu-dō as the prototype against which later *shoin* must be compared.

Yoshimasa may also have used the Dōjin-sai as a room in which to drink tea. There is a hearth for boiling water cut into the floor, and it was recorded by Sōami (?–1525) that tea bowls, whisks, and tea scoops were placed on the staggered shelves. If indeed the shogun did use the Dōjin-sai for tea, it is one of the earliest extant tearooms, and thus of major importance from the point of view not only of the *shoin* style but of the tea ceremony.

29. Staggered shelves and *tsukeshoin* of the Dōjin-sai; Tōgu-dō, Jishō-ji.

The staggered shelves and *tsukeshoin* of the Tōgu-dō are located on the north wall of the Dōjin-sai study. The shelf alcove, half a bay in width, has cupboards with sliding wooden doors at the bottom, and a single-piece shelf (*hiradana*) at the top. The staggered shelves are located at about the center of the alcove and the upper of the two has no retaining molding at its free end. The floorboard of the shelf alcove is equal in height to that of the adjacent *tsukeshoin*, and this contributes to the overall balance of the wall design. The back wall of the *tsukeshoin* is fitted with four sliding wooden doors (*mairado*) with papered backs and two *shōji* screens which can be slid open up to the stops in the lower sill. Above is a transom fit with narrow *shōji* protected on the outside by shutters which can be swung up and fixed open. In all, it is a simple design, but carried out with painstaking care.

THE REIUN-IN SHOIN

The Reiun-in (alternately Ryōun-in) is one of the subtemples of the Zen temple Myōshin-ji. It is the headquarters of the Reiun-ha, one of the four Myōshin-ji subgroups. Located in the western part of the monastery complex and due west of the main abbot's quarters, the Reiun-in may have functioned as a *kohōjō*, or secondary residence of the abbot.

The Reiun-in was begun in 1526 under the direction of the Zen monk Daikyū (1468–1549), but the history and age of the Shoin are unclear. It is known, however, that the emperor Gonara (1496–1557) visited the Shoin, and there is a room within it named the Miyuki no Ma, the Room of the Imperial Sojourn (pl. 30). It is noted in a Myōshin-ji record that the date 1543 was inscribed on the back of a ceiling plank in this room, and that date is often given as that in which the Shoin was constructed. It may be, however, that the Miyuki no Ma was only remodeled in that year in preparation for the emperor.

Whatever the exact date, the Shoin was certainly built in the late Muromachi period, making it the earliest extant structure after the Tōgu-dō to incorporate *shoin*-style elements. More importantly, it is the earliest building extant to include *chōdaigamae* (decorative doors) and the only one of the period to juxtapose *chōdaigamae* and staggered shelves.

The Plan

The main facade of the building faces east and is bounded by a veranda (pl. 31). One enters at this side into the four-and-a-half-mat Tsugi no Ma (anteroom) and then proceeds west to the five-and-a-half-mat Miyuki no Ma, the main room of the structure. Each of these rooms has a secondary three-mat room to the north. A veranda, narrower than that on the east facade, borders the south and west sides as well as half the north.

A *tokonoma* one bay in width has been installed on the north wall of the Tsugi no Ma (pl. 30), and staggered shelves (pl. 32) and a *chōdaigamae* (pl. 33) have been built side by side on the north wall of the main room, the Miyuki no Ma. The separation of *tokonoma* from shelves and *chōdaigamae* is a feature quite different from later *shoin*-style structures.

The Character of the Tokonoma and Staggered Shelves

It will be recalled that the *tokonoma* of the Tōgu-dō was built into an exterior wall, directly opposite the corridor approach. The *tokonoma* of the Reiun-in Shoin is of much the same style as that of the earlier Tōgu-dō but is located in the interior of the building in the Tsugi no Ma, first room west of the veranda. Its dimensions are the same as those of the Tōgu-dō installation, being one bay in width and comparatively shallow in depth. The placement of the *tokonoma* in the Tsugi no Ma is quite representative

59

30. Miyuki no Ma viewed from the Tsugi no Ma;
Reiun-in Shoin, Myōshin-ji.

of the early *shoin* configuration—it was only later that the *tokonoma* and staggered shelves came to be installed side by side. The design here presages later *shoin* styles, though, in that its floor level is low, closer to the level of the *tatami*. The floor of the Tōgu-dō *tokonoma* is, by comparison, raised quite high above the veranda level. Secondly, the *tokonoma* lintel here is raised above the level of the room's mid-wall frieze rail.

The shelf alcove of the Reiun-in Shoin does not incorporate the lower cabinets that are seen in the Tōgu-dō (pl. 29). The upper, single-level shelf (*hiradana*), furthermore, has here been fitted with small sliding panels, making it into an upper cabinet instead (pl. 32). A restraining molding for writing brushes and the like has been added to the Reiun-in shelves. Despite these differences, however, the basic configuration of the shelves themselves is similar in both examples. Interestingly, the shelves here are quite as high as those of the earlier structure despite the absence of the lower cabinets which initially made the shelf height necessary in the Tōgu-dō. Moreover, the floorboard of the Reiun-in shelf alcove is raised and thick, as is the Tōgu-dō example.

Although there is no *tsukeshoin* as such in the Reiun-in Shoin, the single western-most *tatami* mat in front of the shelf alcove is treated differently from the rest of the Miyuki no Ma. All the other mats in the five-and-a-half-mat room are under a single, unpartitioned ceiling, but the ceiling area over the mat in front of the shelves is separated from the rest of the room by ceiling frieze rails and a narrow wall space (*arikabe*)

60

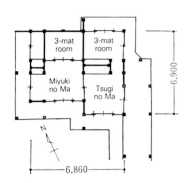

31. Plan of the Reiun-in Shoin, Myō-shin-ji.

32. Staggered shelves of the Miyuki no Ma; Reiun-in Shoin, Myōshin-ji.

above it. A transom in the "bamboo-joint" style over a mid-wall frieze rail helps differentiate the space as well (pls. 30, 33).

These architectural factors indicate that this one-mat area was probably conceived as separate from the rest of the room. It is likely that the space served in place of a built-in *tsukeshoin* and that a movable desk was placed there. The location of the shelves just off the west veranda underscores the plausibility of this study-area hypothesis as well because early shelves and desks were functionally located side by side next to a veranda. The shelves have a bookshelf character like those of the Tōgu-dō.

The Chōdaigamae
The *chōdaigamae* (decorative doors) of the Reiun-in Shoin are the earliest examples still in existence and as such are vitally important to the history of the *shoin* style (pl. 33). Its doors slide on runners, the bottom runner being slightly raised above the level of the *tatami*. Conversely, the upper runner is set somewhat lower than the level of the mid-wall frieze rail. Door jambs divide the two sliding-door panels from the stationary panels (*sodekabe*) at either side. The movable panels open and slide from sight behind these *sodekabe*. This overall form is quite similar to later *chōdaigamae* examples, except that the proportions of the wooden members are thinner and more delicate than in later work.

61

33. *Chōdaigamae* and staggered shelves of the
Miyuki no Ma; Reiun-in Shoin, Myōshin-ji.

The purpose of the room behind the Miyuki no Ma *chōdaigamae* can be conjectured through a comparison of the plan and function of the Reiun-in Shoin with those of later buildings also used for imperial visits. Although this three-mat room is today known as the Gyokuza no Ma (Room of the Jeweled Dais), its three solid and immovable walls recall those of the *nurigome* used in *shinden* houses for sleeping and storage of valuables because of its enclosed and protected nature. Rooms of this type are also found behind the *chōdaigamae* in the audience hall of the Daikaku-ji Guest Hall and in the Jōdan no Ma of the Tsune Goten in the Kyoto Imperial Palace. In both structures, the room behind the *chōdaigamae* is known as the Kenji no Ma (Room of the Sword and Seal). Imperial audiences always took place in front of the room where the sword (*ken*) and seal (*ji*) which accompanied the emperor were located, these being placed on a special shelf (*kenji-dana*) inside that room. If it can be assumed that this custom was in use during the Muromachi period, then it would appear that in the Reiun-in Shoin, this room behind the *chōdaigamae* of the Miyuki no Ma was intended to house imperial regalia. But since the sword and seal were kept at all hours near to the emperor, it seems reasonable to assume that the Kenji no Ma itself developed from the sleeping quarters (*nurigome*) of the *shinden*. This corresponds to the fact that the *chōdaigamae* came into existence as the entrance to sleeping quarters.

The Reiun-in Shoin is therefore of great historical importance. It includes the earliest extant example of an interior *tokonoma* and exhibits an interesting mix of old and new ideas in the *tokonoma* and in the staggered shelves. Furthermore, the Reiun-in Shoin is one of the few remaining structures which incorporates the early form of the *chōdaigamae*, and as such suggests the origins of the *chōdaigamae* itself.

THE SHOIN OF THE YOSHIMIZU SHRINE

Yoshimizu Shrine is located on Mount Yoshino in the southern part of Nara Prefecture, a territory of particularly ancient history. Legends connect the shrine with Minamoto no Yoshitsune (1159–89), the heroic but ill-starred younger brother of the first Kamakura shogun, Yoritomo (1147–99). It was also the residence of the imperial court for a brief time during the period of the so-called Northern and Southern Dynasties (Nambokuchō) in the fourteenth century. The Yoshimizu Shrine was originally known as the Yoshimizu-in, and was a monks' residence belonging to the Kimpusen-ji temple. It became the Yoshimizu Shrine in the early Meiji period (1868–1912) due to the state-sponsored expansion at that time of the Shinto national religion and the separation of the Buddhist and Shinto establishments.

The Shoin of the shrine has been extensively remodeled, the Muromachi-period (1333–1567) structure having been enlarged in the Momoyama period (1568–1614). This Momoyama-period remodeling is thought to have been carried out in 1594 when the great general Toyotomi Hideyoshi (1536–98) stayed at the temple during a cherry blossom festival. It is as yet unclear, however, to what extent the Muromachi-period portion of the building was altered by Hideyoshi. In any case, the Shoin provides glimpses of two quite different styles within the same building.

Yoshitsune's Hiding Place

The main room of the southern half of the Shoin building is known as the Yoshitsune Senkyo no Ma, "Yoshitsune's Hiding Place" (pl. 34). Colorful as the legend may be connecting the Shoin to the young and brilliant conqueror of the Heike clan, the design of the room cannot date to Yoshitsune's lifetime in the late twelfth century. The style is instead of the late Muromachi period, which makes the Yoshitsune Room, together with the Tōgu-dō and the Reiun-in Shoin, a rare extant example of the early *shoin* style.

The *tokonoma* of the twelve-mat room is two bays wide and is located on the main wall (the northern; pl. 35). The *jōdan* of the room, normally a broad area raised one step above the surrounding *tatami* where the host might sit before his guests, is here simply a raised section of *tatami* extending along two bays of the side (east) wall (pls. 35–36). Atop this narrow *jōdan* rests a *tsukeshoin* two bays in length and somewhat more than one foot in width. The staggered shelves are located where this *jōdan-tsukeshoin* fixture meets the north wall.

Although some doubt remains, it appears that the north wall was rebuilt when the Momoyama additions were constructed. It is felt, however, that the style of the

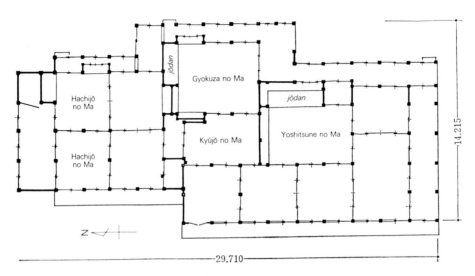

34. Plan of the Shoin, Yoshimizu Shrine.

rebuilt *tokonoma*, staggered shelves, and *tsukeshoin* reflects their original form. Support for this argument lies in the detail, which is of Muromachi appearance.

Tokonoma, Staggered Shelves, Tsukeshoin

The detail of the *tokonoma* reveals the fixture to be of early design. It incorporates thick wooden flooring raised high off the *tatami* beneath, heavy lintel, and shallow depth. The same early elements can be seen in the shelf alcove—in its thick and raised floorboard and fragile, delicate shelves. The *tsukeshoin*, built as a unit with the shelf alcove, retains the height of the shelf alcove floorboard, and both *tsukeshoin* and shelves are built into the *jōdan*, here a "long" two bays in length and one half bay in width.

This grouping of staggered shelves and *tsukeshoin* shows the same study-area quality seen in the western mat of the Miyuki no Ma of the Reiun-in Shoin and in the side-by-side shelves and *tsukeshoin* of the Tōgu-dō Dōjin-sai. The one-unit construction of shelf and *tsukeshoin* desk in the Yoshitsune Room is, together with the basic study-area appearance of the space as a whole, the particularly noteworthy aspect of the room, and shows it to be of early design.

The room does, however, incorporate forward-looking aspects. The *tokonoma* here spans two bays, thus becoming an *ōdoko* ("great *tokonoma*"), popular in later structures. Furthermore, the *tsukeshoin* is now built onto the raised *jōdan* as is the case in mature *shoin* designs.

64

35. *Tokonoma* and staggered shelves of Yoshitsune's Hiding Place; Shoin, Yoshimizu Shrine.

36. *Jōdan* of Yoshitsune's Hiding Place; Shoin, Yoshimizu Shrine.

65

37. *Jōdan* of the Gyokuza no Ma; Shoin,
Yoshimizu Shrine.

The Gyokuza no Ma

The main room of the northern half of the Shoin, the Gyokuza no Ma or "Room of
the Jeweled Dais" (pl. 37), partially abuts on the north wall of the Yoshitsune Room
to the south (pl. 34). Legend has it that the Gyokuza no Ma was used by the emperor
Godaigo (1288–1339), sovereign of the Southern Court at the beginning of the fourteenth century and opponent of Ashikaga Takauji (1305–58), the supporter of the
Northern side and founder of the Ashikaga shogunate. When the temple became a
shrine in the early Meiji period (1868–1912) the spirits of Godaigo and his general
Kusunoki Masashige (1294–1336) were installed as two of the tutelary deities. The
style of the Gyokuza no Ma is, however, clearly of the Momoyama period (1568–
1614), well over two centuries after Godaigo's death. Most probably the room was
constructed for the use of Toyotomi Hideyoshi.

The Gyokuza no Ma affords an opportunity to contrast Muromachi and Momoyama styles within the same building. The *jōdan* of the Gyokuza no Ma occupies the

38. Staggered shelves of the Gyokuza no Ma; Shoin, Yoshimizu Shrine.

northern five of the fifteen mats of the room (pl. 37), more than twice the space allotted the same fixture in the Yoshitsune Room. The wall behind incorporates a *tokonoma* of one and a half bays and beside it, to the west, a one-bay-wide *tokowaki*, a subsidiary *tokonoma* space. A *tsukeshoin* is built into the east veranda wall, and a one-bay-wide shelf alcove into the west (pl. 38).

The *jōdan* of the Gyokuza no Ma no longer presents a study-area quality. It has become instead a place of honor for a personage of high rank, a quality of the *jōdan* in later structures. The juxtaposition of *tokonoma* and *tokowaki* gives the room the appearance of an audience hall in keeping with the new aspect of the *jōdan*. The staggered shelves and *tsukeshoin*, too, are built in a style close to that of mature *shoin* structures. The difference in dates between the northern and southern parts of the building is underscored by the floor configuration as well—in the Gyokuza no Ma the *tatami* mats perfectly fit the dimensions of the floor itself. In the Yoshitsune Room, however, there is a space between the outer *tatami* border and the walls, implying that the floor was originally in the early wooden style, and only later covered by *tatami*. 67

3

SHOIN BUILDINGS
OF THE MOMOYAMA PERIOD

The century of civil war known as the Age of the Country at War gradually came to an end as the struggle among feudal lords for hegemony was resolved by the victories of three successive brilliant generals, Oda Nobunaga (1534–82), Toyotomi Hideyoshi (1536–98), and Tokugawa Ieyasu (1542–1616). The period of stabilization began with Oda Nobunaga's victorious entry into the Kyoto capital in 1568 and the final collapse of the Ashikaga shogunate five years later. The Azuchi Castle built by Nobunaga in 1576 symbolized the strength and vitality of the new order by its massive stone escarpments, towering keep, and gold and polychrome interiors. Its design may have been influenced by knowledge of Western castles and by the advent of firearms, both provided by the Portuguese traders and priests who had first entered the country in 1542 and who enjoyed Nobunaga's favor. Similar fortresses were soon completed by rival daimyo across the country who, undaunted by Nobunaga's success, aspired to national dominance.

After Nobunaga's death, his comrade in arms Toyotomi Hideyoshi came to power and vanquished all remaining enemies, unifying the country for the first time in over one hundred years. Not content with national preeminence, he turned his armies toward China and laid waste to much of Korea before abandoning his hopes for empire.

Hideyoshi's artistic inclinations were equally grandiose, attested by his great building schemes at the Osaka Castle, Juraku-dai castle-palace, and Fushimi (or popularly Momoyama) Castle. It was the last that gave its name to this short era (1568–1614) of stabilization in government and brilliant creativity in the visual arts. Hideyoshi, fond of massive entertainments, sponsored a grandiose tea ceremony at Kitano, to which the entire population of Kyoto was invited, and his cherry-blossom viewing excursion in south Kyoto prompted the reconstruction of the Sambō-in, dealt with further on in this chapter.

Hideyoshi's period of ascendency was marked by flourishing foreign trade and great artistic activity at home. Sen no Rikyū (1522–91) and Furuta Oribe (1543–1615) perfected the ceremony of tea and the aesthetic code of simplicity and astringency it entails (see Chapter Five). Simultaneously, Kanō Eitoku (1543–90), Hasegawa Tōhaku

(1539–1610), Unkoku Tōgan (1547–1618), and Kaihō Yūshō (1533–1615) competed with each other in creating vigorous and brilliant *fusuma* paintings in gold and polychrome to decorate the mansions of their patrons. The *shoin* style of architecture cannot be considered but in the context of both these differing aesthetic schemes—the restrained "tea taste" and the lavish decorative programs of the great mansions.

After Hideyoshi's death, his one-time ally Tokugawa Ieyasu brought to completion the national unification process after the epic battles at Sekigahara in 1600 and at Osaka Castle in 1615. His founding of the Tokugawa shogunate marks the end of the Momoyama period and the beginning of a new political and cultural order named the Edo period after his selection of the fishing town of Edo as the capital of his military regime.

Extant Momoyama Structures

The general characteristics of *shoin* structures in the Momoyama period can be gleaned from the thirty-four extant examples that have been designated National Treasures or Important Cultural Properties by the Japanese government. These buildings fall generally into two categories. The first are those that function as guest halls (*kyakuden*), many of which bear such names as *shoin* or *shinden* (宸殿), the latter meaning "imperial apartments" and not to be confused with the Heian *shinden* (寝殿). The second is the abbot's quarters (*hōjō*) type, also incorporating structures labeled *hondō* ("main hall") and *kuri* (Zen temple kitchens, often with sleeping quarters and guest rooms as well). The most important of these thirty-four date from the later part of the Momoyama period (1568–1614), perhaps due to the somewhat more peaceful conditions prevalent among religious establishments during these years. Sadly, however, no examples of the warrior residence (*buke-zukuri*) survive from the Momoyama era.

The extant Momoyama structures still show in their plans and interiors the early *shoin* style. It is consequently accurate to suggest that the mature *shoin* does not fully develop until later, in the beginning of the Edo period. These Momoyama structures do, however, present the first opportunity to examine fully the development of the four main interior elements of the *shoin* style—the *tokonoma*, staggered shelves, *tsuke-shoin*, and *chōdaigamae*. It is here that the ideas tentatively applied in the late Muromachi structures surpass the preparatory stage and come to be widely incorporated into building schemes. Most importantly, it is at this time that the grouping of the four main elements in a prescribed scheme in the main room becomes one of the standard arrangements for upper-class dwellings.

The Front Shoin of the Sambō-in

The Sambō-in is a building complex first constructed in 1115 by Shōkaku (1057–1129), the fourteenth abbot of Daigo-ji temple, the headquarters of the Daigo-ji 69 branch of the Shingon Buddhist sect. It is not, however, simply a subtemple of Daigo-ji, but rather a major Shingon temple in its own right. In fact, the Sambō-in *monzeki* (abbot of noble blood) administers the entire Daigo-ji as well, following a tradition established in the middle ages.

The present Sambō-in is located in the northwest sector of the Daigo-ji compound. The old Sambō-in was lost in the Ōnin war (1467–77), and a temple complex called the Kongōrin-in was later built on the site. This, in turn, was renovated beginning in 1598 and the original name of Sambō-in was restored. This renovation was under-taken in preparation for Toyotomi Hideyoshi's Daigo-ji cherry blossom viewing. Some believe that Hideyoshi himself ordered the rebuilding of the old Kongōrin-in structures.

Details concerning the Keichō-era (1596–1615) reconstruction of the Sambō-in are found in the *Gien jugō nikki*, the diary of Gien (1558–1626), abbot of Daigo-ji at the time. According to this source, the renovation work was by and large completed by 1613. Although parts of the complex have since been altered, it is reasonably certain that the Front Shoin (Omote Shoin) and the other important structures date from about that time (pl. 39). The Front Shoin and the attached Chokushi no Ma complex are formal public areas, whereas the Imperial Apartments are of a more private function. The Shiroshoin is the living quarters for the abbot, and the Kuri is the kitchen area. These structures have all been designated Important Cultural Properties, as has the "Chinese" Gate (Karamon), the south entrance, which was originally located on the west wall and named the Heichū-mon. This gate is in the *hira-karamon* style, characterized by a roof which employs bowed "Chinese" gables (*karahafu*) on both ends (pl. 40).

The complex also includes a superlative garden and pond at the south side (pl. 41). The best gardeners in the capital were assembled for its construction, and Hide-yoshi's enthusiasm for the project was such that he had a particularly famous stone moved there from his own Juraku-dai castle-palace. After Hideyoshi died, Gien saw the project through to completion.

When first built, the present Front Shoin was known as the Shinden (Sleeping Hall). Although some points regarding the construction of this building are unclear, it is important in that its unique plan shows a number of early *shoin*-style charac-teristics.

Characteristics of the Plan
One enters the Front Shoin by the main entrance at the west and proceeds through three large rooms aligned west to east: the San no Ma (twenty-seven mats), the Ni no Ma (eighteen mats), and the Ichi no Ma (fifteen mats; pl. 42). A veranda extends the length of the south side, bordering on the garden. The west end of the veranda abuts on a *chūmon-rō*, a short, covered entrance arcade, which here projects into the garden in a fashion reminiscent of the "fountain pavilion" of the *shinden* style. An

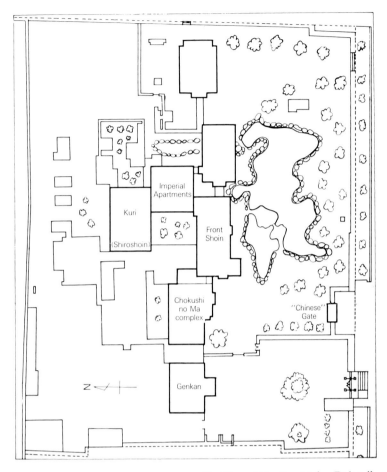

39. Plan of the Sambō-in, Daigo-ji.

inner corridor extends from this *chūmon-rō* along the west and north sides of the structure. Extending around all four sides are outer verandas, which are one step lower than the wide southern veranda and have ornamental railings. Wooden steps with the same type of railings provide access to the garden at the center of the south facade and at the western entrance just north of the *chūmon-rō*. Paneled Chinese-style doors and a curved "Chinese" gable give visual emphasis to the western entrance.

The plan of the Front Shoin, with its single row of rooms and *chūmon-rō* projecting into the garden, was old-fashioned for its day and no other contemporary buildings with this layout are extant. But more up-to-date elements were incorporated into the design as well. A *jōdan* is included, and a *tokonoma* and staggered shelves were added as well, producing *in toto* the effect of the *shoin* audience hall.

The exterior appearance of the Front Shoin also reflects contemporary trends insofar as the *chūmon-rō* and reticulated shutters (*shitomido*), Chinese-style paneled doors (*sankarado*) and "Chinese" gable (*karahafu*), all closely relate to those of the Kangaku-in and the Kōjō-in guest halls of Onjō-ji, two buildings nearly coeval with the Sambō-in that are discussed later in this chapter. Finally, a structure for viewing the Nō drama is said to have been moved to this Shoin, but it was most likely used as a hall for holding interviews.

40. "Chinese" Gate, Sambō-in, Daigo-ji.

41. South facade and garden of the Front Shoin; Sambō-in, Daigo-ji.

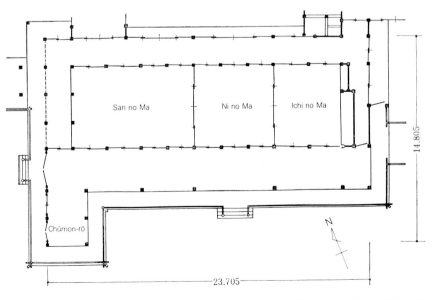

42. Plan of the Front Shoin; Sambō-in, Daigo-ji.

The Chokushi no Ma Complex

To the west of the Front Shoin is a structure comprised of three handsome rooms aligned east to west (pls. 39, 43): the Chokushi no Ma (Imperial Envoy Room), Akigusa no Ma (Autumn Grasses Room), and the Aoi no Ma (Hollyhock Room). These were built at the same time as the Front Shoin and likewise are designated Important Cultural Properties. As is the case with the Front Shoin, the three rooms are arranged in a single line on an east to west axis, and only the easternmost room, the Chokushi no Ma, has a *tokonoma*. The *tokonoma* here retains the thick *oshiita* floorboard, the front edge of which is exposed to view. This is opposed to later *tokonoma*, which tend to employ a thinner floorboard with a thick, decorative molding (*tokogamachi*) on the facing edge. The lintel of this *tokonoma*, however, has a newer design, being positioned quite high above the *tatami*. The *tokonoma* is the only extant example that incorporates on its back wall wainscoted *shōji* screens of the kind usually found behind *tsukeshoin* (writing desks).

The Chokushi no Ma is connected to the Front Shoin by a corridor of such beauty that it is classified as an Important Cultural Property. One square bay in measure and roofed with a curved "Chinese" gable (*karahafu*), it recalls the *ochima* of the *shinden* style, a small corridor with a low floor. In the middle of the veranda to the south of the Chokushi no Ma is a stairway with ornamental railing. Above it rests a second "Chinese" gable. The Chokushi no Ma thus functions much like an entryway-waiting room, and the progression from this through the *ochima* corridor to the Front Shoin recalls the *shinden*-style plan.

Stylistic Advances in the Front Shoin

The *jōdan* of the Front Shoin is quite large, consisting of the entire Ichi no Ma and Ni no Ma combined (pl. 44). On the east wall of the Ichi no Ma are installed a *tokonoma* adjacent to the south veranda and staggered shelves beside it to the north (pl. 50). The *tokonoma* is very wide, especially when compared to those of the Tōgu-dō and Reiun-in Shoin, and is deeper as well. The lintel, moreover, is higher than in previous examples. A trend toward the enlargement of the *tokonoma* space is thus seen in the Front Shoin. The *tokonoma* style is also advanced in that it no longer employs the thick, one-piece *oshiita* floorboard seen in earlier examples, but rather incorporates a lacquered decorative molding (*tokogamachi*), a characteristic of later *tokonoma* designs. The addition of a *kamachi* is another characteristic of later designs. On the other hand, the marked thickness of the lintel still reflects early design ideas. The same is true in the retention here of a *kegomiita*, a thin section of wall below the floorboard and above the *tatami*. Later *tokonoma* will be seen to incorporate thinner lintels and to dispense with the *kegomiita*.

The staggered shelves of the Front Shoin do, in fact, eliminate the *kegomiita*, with the decorative molding instead resting directly on the *tatami* mats (pls. 44, 50). The shelf alcove is wider than previous examples as well, and is the earliest seen in this

74

survey to utilize a tripartite design, the shelves being no longer simply set on two different levels but rather incorporating a raised central piece between lower flanking sections. This design, known as *seirō-dana*, is also seen in the Gyokuza no Ma of the Yoshimizu Shrine, also thought built for the use of Hideyoshi (pl. 38). As was the case with the *tokonoma*, however, the shelves are retardataire in that they are still raised quite high above the floorboard.

Along with these various changes in detail, the interior elements of the Front Shoin show a marked change in overall positioning and in architectural purpose. The entire Ichi no Ma and Ni no Ma have been combined to form the *jōdan* and thus to accommodate a larger number of people. This is a functional and stylistic advance from Yoshitsune's Hiding Place wherein the *jōdan* was simply an addition within the *shoin* room (pls. 35–36). This is the style used in many mature large-scale *shoin* structures.

The most significant departure from the previous styles, however, is seen in the arrangement of the *tokonoma* and staggered shelves. As opposed to the Tōgu-dō, Reiun-in Shoin, and Yoshimizu Shrine Shoin, there is no *tsukeshoin* in the Ichi no Ma of the Front Shoin. The shelves here are linked, not to a *tsukeshoin*, but to the *tokonoma*. The interior elements, consequently, no longer give the impression of being related to study purposes, which require close proximity of *tsukeshoin* and shelves. Instead, the staggered shelves have assumed a purely decorative function, becoming one of the set elements of the main room. Concurrently, the *tokonoma* has been moved into the main room as was the case at the Yoshimizu Shrine Shoin, and is no longer an element of the secondary spaces. In sum, the *tokonoma* and staggered shelves have been incorporated on the main wall of the most important room and been used there for primarily decorative effect. The interior of the Front Shoin thus constitutes a marked advance toward the mature *shoin* style. The use of ceiling battens (*saobuchi*), grill transom (*osa-ramma*), and stylistically advanced *fusuma* paintings is likewise close to later *shoin* ideas (pl. 44). This is in opposition to the exterior, which recalls the earlier *shinden* style in its *chūmon-rō* corridor, reticulated shutters (*shitomido*), and ornamental railings on outer verandas (pl. 41).

THE SAMBŌ-IN IMPERIAL APARTMENTS

The Sambō-in Imperial Apartments (宸殿; *shinden*) are connected to the Front Shoin at its northeast corner, this position suggesting the more private nature of the structure (pl. 39). Although the general plan of the building indicates a date of construction close to that of the Front Shoin, around 1598, some scholars attribute it on the basis of various interior elements to a slightly later date, sometime in the Kan'ei era (1624–44).

Characteristics of the Plan
The Imperial Apartments have a square plan with four rooms of nearly equal size

occupying one corner each (pl. 45). The main room, the Jōza Ichi no Ma, is in the northeast, and beside it to the northwest is the Mushakakushi no Ma ("Warriors' Hiding Place"). The Ni no Ma and San no Ma are to the southeast and southwest repectively. Three of the four sides of the structures are bordered with broad verandas (*hiroen*) and outer verandas one step lower (*ochien*), save where the building abuts on the temple kitchens.

The most noteworthy of the rooms in the Imperial Apartments is the ten-mat Jōza Ichi no Ma, which includes a *tokonoma* one and a half bays wide, and bordering it to the west, one-bay-wide staggered shelves (pls. 46, 51). At the east, a *tsukeshoin* projects into the veranda, and at the west a *chōdaigamae* (partially visible in plate 51) leads to the Mushakakushi no Ma—an assemblage that corresponds almost exactly to the mature *shoin* configuration. The only stylistically lagging element is a one-half-bay section of wall on the western side between the *chōdaigamae* and the staggered shelves to the north. This fixed wall corresponds to the side of the *tokonoma* in the adjoining Mushakakushi no Ma (pl. 45). Mature *shoin* rooms do not show this section of wall, and it interrupts the otherwise well-developed *shoin* system of the Jōza Ichi no Ma.

It is open to question whether the name Mushakakushi no Ma is coeval with the date of construction (pl. 47). The elements of the room seem not for "bodyguard concealing" as the name implies, but rather for contributing to a living-area atmosphere. This is true of the *tokonoma* built into the east side of the north wall and the *tsukeshoin* located diagonally across at the south side of the west. The living area function of the room is implied as well by the *chōdaigamae*, which originally served as the entrance from a more formal room, like the Jōza Ichi no Ma, to a private sleeping area.

In light of these characteristics of the Jōza Ichi no Ma and the Mushakakushi no Ma, it is clear that the Imperial Apartments have a more private nature than the Front Shoin, which was seen to evoke a formal, audience hall atmosphere.

Interior Elements of the Jōza Ichi no Ma
The staggered shelves and *tsukeshoin* are the elements of the Jōza Ichi no Ma which make the most marked departure from earlier designs. Like those of the Front Shoin, the shelves here (pl. 48) use a lacquered molding (*kamachi*) which rests directly on the *tatami* with no intervening wall space (*kegomiita*). Above the shelves are installed cabinets with sliding panels. The cabinets are of a lower height than in older shelf styles. The two-level shelves are of quite original design and are popularly known as Daigo Shelves (*daigo-dana*). They are not fixed to the back wall of the alcove but rather stand in front of it, being fixed in place at the side walls and supported at the center by a thin column which rests on the alcove floorboard. Retaining backs, carved with delicate openwork designs, have been fixed to the shelves as well. These Daigo Shelves, plus the Mist Shelves (*kasumi-dana;* pl. 157) of the Shugaku-in Detached

76

Palace and the Katsura Shelves (*katsura-dana;* pl. 151) of the Katsura Detached Palace, constitute the Three Supreme Shelves in *shoin* architecture. The Kuroshoin of Nishi Hongan-ji incorporates Daigo Shelves as well (pl. 143), but there are stylistic differences between them that reflect different dates of construction.

The advanced elements of the *tsukeshoin* are the low sliding panels beneath the writing surface and the ogee-arched window (*katōmado*) illuminating it (pl. 46). *Tsukeshoin* with ogee-arched windows come to be frequently seen in later *shoin* architecture. The lower half of the window here, however, is fitted with high wainscoting, a feature characteristic of earlier, less mature designs. The transom of this *tsukeshoin* is worth mention as well for its delicate flower and diamond latticework.

The *tokonoma* exhibits both up-to-date and retardataire features. The laquered facing (*kamachi*), resting directly on the *tatami*, and the low level of the floorboard reflect advanced designs, but the thickness of the lintel is still quite marked, as in early examples. In sum, the *tokonoma*, staggered shelves, and *tsukeshoin* have become decorations for the main room, and have progressed toward the styles of the Edo period.

The advanced elements of the interior do cast some doubt on the Keichō-era (1596–1615) attribution of the Imperial Apartments. Nonetheless, the configuration of the plan and the absence of the roughly finished posts (*menkawa-bashira*) characteristic of later buildings such as the Kuroshoin of Nishi Hongan-ji indicate an earlier date, probably near that of the Front Shoin. The advanced design of the interior, as compared to the style of the Front Shoin, may have resulted from the differing functions intended for the two structures.

Shiroshoin

Another group of rooms of historical interest in the Sambō-in are located in the rear part of the temple kitchens (the Kuri). These seven rooms are known as the Shiroshoin, and although parts were rebuilt in later years, it is nevertheless a structure worthy of note. Although the rooms are now used as the residence of the abbot, their original function is not precisely known. At the north, a room of seven and a half mats and another of three mats are arranged side by side (pl. 49). The north wall of the larger room includes a three-tiered cabinet with two pairs of *fusuma* panels on each tier. The three-mat room includes shelves of complex design. These elements suggest the structure served as an area for study and daily living.

The Sambō-in complex is particularly valuable historically because it well represents the appearance of a *monzeki* temple of the late Momoyama period, a temple of a priest related to the imperial house or one of a number of specific noble families. Examination of it leads to an appreciation of the constituent parts of each building and of each building to the whole. It is a fine example of one direction of *shoin* development.

77

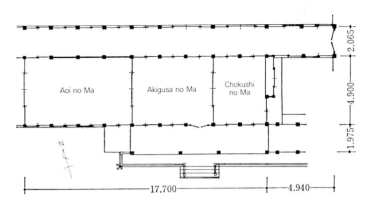

43. Plan of the Chokushi no Ma complex; Sambō-in, Daigo-ji.

44. *Jōdan* (Ichi no Ma and Ni no Ma) of the Front Shoin; Sambō-in, Daigo-ji.

45. Plan of the Imperial Apartments; Sambō-in, Daigo-ji.

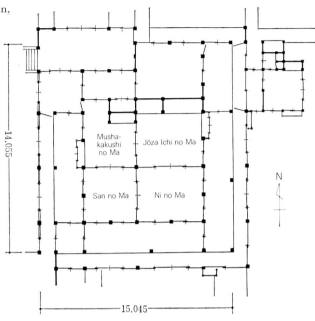

46. *Tokonoma*, staggered shelves, and *tsukeshoin* of the Jōza Ichi no Ma; Imperial Apartments, Sambō-in, Daigo-ji.

47. *Tokonoma* and *chōdaigamae* of the
Mushakakushi no Ma; Imperial
Apartments, Sambō-in, Daigo-ji.

49. Partial view of the Shiroshoin, Sambō-in, Daigo-ji.

48. Staggered shelves of the Jōza
Ichi no Ma; Imperial Apartments,
Sambō-in, Daigo-ji.

50. Jōdan Ichi no Ma of the Front Shoin;
Sambō-in, Daigo-ji.
The main wall of the Front Shoin Ichi no Ma
is fitted with a *tokonoma* and staggered shelves.
It is this arrangement that becomes standard
for subsequent structures and not the *tsukeshoin*-
shelf combination of the Tōgu-dō. The shelves
are in the tripartite *seirō-dana* style, and cupboards with elegantly painted panels are installed above. The shelves are here becoming
primarily decorative in function.

51. Jōza Ichi no Ma of the Imperial Apartments; Sambō-in, Daigo-ji.

The Jōza Ichi no Ma has a mature *shoin* design with *tokonoma* and staggered shelves on the main wall, and *tsukeshoin* and *chōdaigamae* to either side. The *daigo-dana* shelves and ogee-arched window of the *tsukeshoin* are intricately crafted, and the small cupboards with sliding panels are a new element in *tsukeshoin* design. The *chōdaigamae*, however, retains its original function as the entrance to a sleeping area.

THE KŌJŌ-IN GUEST HALL

The Kōjō-in is a subtemple of Onjō-ji, a temple complex six miles to the east of Kyoto in Ōtsu City on the shores of Lake Biwa. Onjō-ji, popularly known as Mii-dera, is the headquarters of the Jimon sect of Tendai Buddhism, and long the most important sanctuary in the provinces around Lake Biwa. The seventeenth-century Onjō-ji included, besides the Kōjō-in Guest Hall, two others important to the history of *shoin* architecture. One is the Guest Hall of the Kangaku-in, still on the Onjō-ji grounds. The other was once part of the former Nikkō-in and was later moved to the Gokoku-ji temple in Tokyo where it is known as the Gakkō-den. All three are important extant examples of the early *shoin* style, but are individually distinguished by differences in plan.

The Kōjō-in is believed to have been established in the Muromachi period by a powerful rural samurai family, the Yamaoka, whose members supported it for generations, until 1603. The present Guest Hall is thought to have been built in 1601. The plan of the building (pl. 54) closely resembles the "*shuden* plan" (pl. 55) in the five-volume *Shōmei*, a builder's guide compiled in 1608 by Heinouchi Masanobu as a secret compendium of the building techniques of the Heinouchi family, hereditary builders to the Edo shogunate. Because of the close correspondence, the Kōjō-in Guest Hall is considered an archetypical example of the style of building called the *shuden*, literally "principal hall." Until recently this *shuden* style was thought to be an independent building style, but current consensus is rather that the *shuden* style, and thus the Guest Hall of the Kōjō-in, is not an independent building type but instead an early phase of the *shoin* style. Because the inscription on the *Shōmei* illustration reads "Plan of an *Old* Six-Bay-by-Seven-Bay Shuden" (italics added), the design depicted is thought to be representative of a late Muromachi-period style, popular well before the diagram was executed in 1608. This implies that the Guest Hall of the Kōjō-in, closest among extant *shoin* structures to the *Shōmei* design, must have been in plan somewhat retardataire from the outset.

The Plan

The main facade of the Guest Hall (pl. 56) faces east, with an entry arcade (*chūmon-rō*) at the southeast corner. A broad veranda extends from this *chūmon-rō* to the west along the south side (pl. 57), and an outer veranda surrounds the entire structure. This outer veranda connects to a second broad veranda at the northeast, joining the building to the temple kitchens. Two rows of rooms are arranged parallel to the south veranda (pl. 54). The south row is comprised of, from the west, the Jōza no Ma (eighteen mats), the Tsugi no Ma (eighteen mats), and the Saya no Ma (six mats). The north row contains, again from the west, the Nando (six mats), the Hachijō no Ma (eight mats), the Jūnijō no Ma (twelve mats), and another Saya no Ma (four mats). The Guest Hall is thus a rough square composed of four major spaces, considering the Nando and Hachijō no Ma to be a single unit and the two Saya no Ma to be foyers to the two larger eastern rooms. The most important of them is the Jōza no Ma.

Although the configuration of the Kōjō-in Guest Hall relates in general quite closely to that of the *shuden* plan in the *Shōmei*, there are a number of divergences which should be pointed out (pls. 54–55). The *jōdan* of the Kōjō-in Guest Hall is smaller in area than that of the *shuden* rendering, and the west side is not a shelf space as in the corresponding area of the *shuden jōdan* but rather a *tokonoma*. Second, although both plans include on the north side a *nando*, a fixed-wall subsidiary room, the Guest Hall divides the space so as to include the Hachijō no Ma as well. Also, the northwest room of the Guest Hall, the Jūnijō no Ma, does not include the *tokonoma* or the shelves shown in the *Shōmei* design. Finally, the Guest Hall incorporates many more *shitomido* on the east facade but does not include a formal entrance area (*shikidai*). The absence of the *shikidai* in the Guest Hall may be due to its direct connection to the temple kitchens. The *shuden* in the *Shōmei* is, conversely, an independent structure, thus needing an entryway of its own. The difference may also relate to the fact that the Kōjō-in Guest Hall is a temple structure whereas the *shuden* plan relates more to a warrior mansion with correspondingly greater need for a large and formal entryway.

Despite these differences in detail, however, the two buildings are very close in general conception. The Kōjō-in Guest Hall is thus immensely valuable as an extant example of an "old six-bay-by-seven-bay *shuden*." The successor of this style, the *hiroma*, is also represented in the *Shōmei* and will be discussed further on in the chapter.

The Jōza no Ma
Description of the Jōza no Ma must begin with the one-bay-square *jōdan* which projects into the south veranda from the southwest corner of the room (pls. 52, 54, 58). The *tsukeshoin*, one bay in width, is located at the south of this and gives the space a suggestion of a study area. A one-bay *tokonoma* is built into the western wall. This *jōdan* space is quite similar to that of the guest hall of the former Nikkō-in, and in general is quite characteristic of early *shoin* designs.

The main wall (the western) of the Jōza no Ma proper exhibits a two-bay *tokonoma* flanked to the north by shelves one bay wide (pl. 60). Adjacent to this on the north wall is a two-bay *chōdaigamae* (pl. 59). This arrangement is seen in both the Front Shoin and Imperial Apartments of the Sambō-in, and is, like the *jōdan* area, characteristic of Momoyama-period designs.

The major element of the Jōza no Ma that distinguishes the Kōjō-in Guest Hall from the other two *shoin* buildings originally at the Onjō-ji, the Kangaku-in and the former Nikkō-in Guest Halls, is the presence here of *chōdaigamae* doors (pl. 59). Their position in the room, furthermore, foreshadows later *chōdaigamae* types. The type has become formalized here, suggesting that a shift from the purely functional to the decorative is continuing to take place. A problem with the arrangement, though, lies

52. *Jōdan* of the Jōza no Ma; Kōjō-in Guest Hall, Onjō-ji.

The layout of the Kōjō-in Guest Hall closely resembles that of the *"shuden* plan" in the *Shōmei*, a builder's guide from the Edo period, and is consequently considered an important example of the early *shoin* style. Both incorporate a small subsidiary area with a raised floor projecting into a veranda from the main audience hall. In the Kōjō-in Guest Hall, this space incorporates a *tsukeshoin* and a *tokonoma*, recalling the study areas of Muromachi-period dwellings. The corresponding space in the *"shuden* plan" has an even more pronounced study-area quality because the *tsukeshoin* is flanked not by a *tokonoma* but by shelves.

53. Jōza Ichi no Ma of the Kangaku-in Guest Hall, Onjō-ji.
Although an audience hall, the Jōza Ichi no Ma has a very simple design, incorporating only a great *tokonoma* on its main wall. Nevertheless, the dazzling gold and polychrome wall painting lends a Momoyama magnificence to the space. Depicting a waterfall among clouds, the painting was done by Kanō Mitsunobu (1561–1608), who took over the leadership of the Kanō school, hereditary painters to the shogunate, upon the death of his father, the great Eitoku (1543–90).

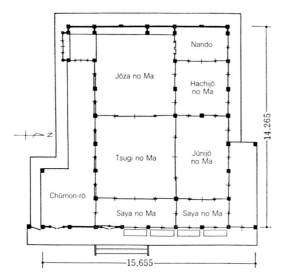

54. Plan of the Kōjō-in Guest Hall, Onjō-ji.

in the inclusion of two rooms behind the *chōdaigamae* (pl. 54). This requires a partition which bisects the space behind the doors in a most unnatural manner. It is questionable indeed whether this design is original. The presence of a *nando* behind the *chōdaigamae*, though, does reflect the original function of the doors as an entrance to private quarters.

The trend from the functional to the decorative is seen as well in the *jōdan* area (pl. 58). Although the space as a whole retains the atmosphere of a study area, the wall to the west of the *tsukeshoin* contains no staggered shelves here but rather a *tokonoma*, an element more completely for decorative display than are staggered shelves. The *jōdan* space consequently is changing from a pure study area to one which could be used as well as a waiting room or relaxation area. This type of *jōdan* is frequently seen in later *shoin*-style buildings, especially in the private *shoin* of temple complexes.

A number of old-style elements remain, however, in these apartments. The two-bay *tokonoma* retains the old *oshiita* style, with high flooring, thick lintel, and shallow depth (pl. 60). The staggered shelves show the same style as those in the Sambō-in Front Shoin, having a delicate flavor recalling early designs (pl. 50). The alcove floor is somewhat lower than that of the *tokonoma*, and the shelves, set at middle height in the alcove, exhibit the tripartite *seirō-dana* style in which the central section is raised a step above the flanking pair. The old style is retained on the exterior of the building as well, in the extensive use of reticulated shutters (*shitomido*). The Guest Hall of the former Nikkō-in uses many *shitomido* as well.

The Kōjō-in Guest Hall is thus important as an extant example of the *shuden*-type *shoin* of the late Muromachi period. Its use of hipped-and-gabled roof, *chūmon-rō* with pitched roof, and projecting *jōdan* are typical of this style, as is the bow-shaped "Chinese" gable (*karahafu*) shielding an entrance porch (*kurumayose*) and wooden swinging doors.

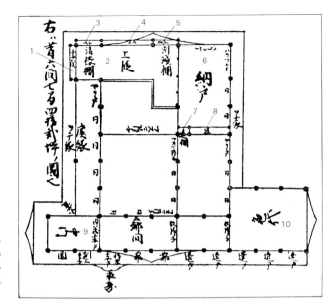

55. "*Shuden* plan" (from the Heino-uchi *Shōmei*): 1) *tsukeshoin*, 2) *jōdan*, 3) staggered shelves, 4) *tokonoma*, 5) staggered shelves, 6) Nando, 7) staggered shelves, 9) Chūmon-rō, 10) Shikidai.

56. East facade of the Kōjō-in Guest Hall, Onjō-ji.

57. South facade (exterior of the *jōdan* and Jōza no Ma) of the Kōjō-in Guest Hall, Onjō-ji.

58. *Jōdan* of the Jōza no Ma; Kōjō-in Guest Hall, Onjō-ji.

59. Jōza no Ma viewed from the Tsugi no Ma;
Kōjō-in Guest Hall, Onjō-ji.

60. *Tokonoma* and staggered shelves
of the Jōza no Ma; Kōjō-in Guest
Hall, Onjō-ji.

THE KANGAKU-IN GUEST HALL

The Kangaku-in, like the previously discussed Kōjō-in, is a subtemple of the Tendai temple of Onjō-ji on Lake Biwa. It serves as the Onjō-ji study center. According to an ink inscription of 1799 on the wall boards of the *tokonoma*, the Guest Hall of the Kangaku-in was constructed in 1600 by the great daimyo Mōri Terumoto (1553–1625) at the behest of Toyotomi Hideyori (1593–1615), second son of Hideyoshi. The inscription is corroborated by the notation "1600, fifth month" discovered on the back of the bamboo-joint motif atop the veranda partition at the south end of the facade. Furthermore, the entry for the fourth month, twenty-eighth day of 1601 in the *Gien jugō nikki*, the diary of the abbot Gien, mentions the Kangaku-in Guest Hall, which proves the building to have been completed by 1601 and corroborates the inscriptions dating the construction of the Guest Hall to 1600.

The Kangaku-in Guest Hall and the Shuden Plan

The main facade of the Guest Hall faces east (pl. 61). A covered entrance arcade (*chūmon-rō*) connects to the broad veranda extending the length of the south side. The interior is arranged in three rows of rooms parallel to this south veranda (pl. 62). A second broad veranda borders the east sides of the Hachijō no Ma and the Tsuru no Ma and abuts on the Saya no Ma at the south. Beyond the broad veranda is an outer veranda which skirts all four sides of the building. The exterior of Kangaku-in Guest Hall is very close in design to that of the Kōjō-in, exhibiting the same *shuden*-style *chūmon-rō* and entry porch (*kurumayose*) with bow-shaped "Chinese" gable. It also uses the *shinden*-style reticulated shutters (*shitomido*), though to a lesser extent than does the Kōjō-in Guest Hall.

Like the Guest Hall of the Kōjō-in, the Kangaku-in Guest Hall has a plan (pl. 62) reflected in the *Shōmei* compendium of the Heinouchi family building techniques. The rendering therein, entitled "Plan of a Contemporary Hiroma" (pl. 63), shows the same three-row plan, with *chūmon-rō*, entry porch (*kurumayose*) with a bow-shaped "Chinese" gable, and south veranda. The notation "contemporary" implies that the larger *hiroma* plan was in use in 1608, the year from which the *Shōmei* dates. It is, thus, a later design than that of the Kōjō-in Guest Hall and the "*shuden* plan" which was, it will be recalled, described by Heinouchi in 1608 as an "old" plan. This "Plan of a Contemporary Hiroma" is in fact very close to the mature *shoin* plan of the Ōhiroma complex in the Ninomaru Palace of Nijō Castle, to be discussed in the following chapter.

The three-row plan is, however, not seen in the other two aforementioned Onjō-ji *shoin* buildings, the guest halls of the Kōjō-in and the former Nikkō-in. That the Kangaku-in Guest Hall incorporates three rows of rooms may have been due to its special function as a study center in which a large number of monks would gather, thus necessitating the extra space.

93

61. East facade of the Kangaku-in Guest Hall, Onjō-ji.

Stylistic Variation in the Interior

The Jōza Ichi no Ma seems to have been the formal audience hall because of its grandiose appearance and attached anteroom which usually accompanies a main audience space (pl. 64). The main wall of the Jōza Ichi no Ma is occupied entirely by a two-bay *tokonoma* (pl. 53). Staggered shelves and *tsukeshoin* are absent. Apparently there was no need to appoint the room with all the design elements normally associated with the *shoin* scheme. Because the structure had had no residential function, there was no need for a fixed-wall room for storage or sleeping (*nando*) or the usual decorative doors (*chōdaigamae*) opening into it. This is a different design from the three-row Ōhiroma of the Ninomaru Palace at Nijō Castle, which retains the *chōdaigamae* and fixed-wall room behind. All the interior partitions in the Kangaku-in Guest Hall are instead *fusuma*.

The *tokonoma* of the Jōza Ichi no Ma is of an old style (pl. 53). The floorboard is a simple *oshiita*, a *kegomiita* is installed beneath, and the lintel is thick. To provide visual compensation for the great width of the *tokonoma*, the lintel is set at a high level and the floorboard is very thick as well. The fact that the entire main wall is taken up by

94

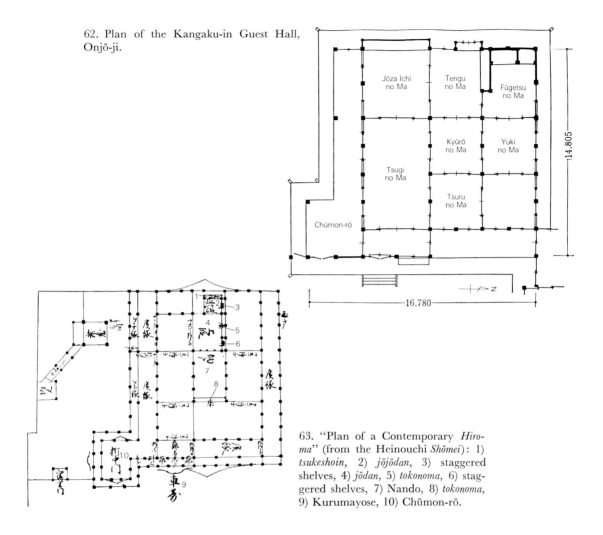

62. Plan of the Kangaku-in Guest Hall, Onjō-ji.

Jōza Ichi no Ma

Tengu no Ma

Fūgetsu no Ma

Kyūrō no Ma

Yuki no Ma

Tsugi no Ma

Tsuru no Ma

Chūmon-rō

14.805

16.780

z

63. "Plan of a Contemporary *Hiroma*" (from the Heinouchi *Shōmei*): 1) *tsukeshoin*, 2) *jōjōdan*, 3) staggered shelves, 4) *jōdan*, 5) *tokonoma*, 6) staggered shelves, 7) Nando, 8) *tokonoma*, 9) Kurumayose, 10) Chūmon-rō.

a *tokonoma* reflects the importance that the *tokonoma* has assumed at this stage in the development of the *shoin* style.

To the north of the Jōza Ichi no Ma is the Tengu no Ma, a room including a *tokonoma* of one and a half bays on its north wall, and a *tsukeshoin* one bay wide adjacent to it on the west wall (pl. 65). The style of this *tokonoma* is much like that of the Jōza Ichi no Ma, but because of its narrower dimensions the floorboard here is thinner and the lintel lower than on the Jōza Ichi no Ma example. The design of the *tsukeshoin* is of an early nature too, but the four-panel scheme of the wainscoted *shōji* behind it becomes the basic one for later writing alcoves. The Tengu no Ma is by comparison to the Jōza Ichi no Ma more private in nature, as expressed by the *fusuma* which are painted in ink monochrome and not brilliant gold.

The private orientation seen in the Tengu no Ma is true as well for the Fūgetsu no Ma in the northwest corner of the building. It includes a *tokonoma* and a cabinet in its west wall. This Fūgetsu no Ma is, however, a rebuilt version. It is true, though, that originally it was of a private nature as well. The inclusion of private rooms along with the public Jōza Ichi no Ma under one roof is perhaps another reason for the adoption of a three-row plan.

95

64. Jōza Ichi no Ma viewed from the
Ni no Ma; Kangaku-in Guest Hall,
Onjō-ji.

65. *Tokonoma* and *tsukeshoin* of the
Tengu no Ma; Kangaku-in Guest
Hall, Onjō-ji.

The Kanchi-in Guest Hall

The Kanchi-in is a subtemple within the compound of the great Kyōōgokoku-ji (familiarly known as Tō-ji), the headquarters of the Tō-ji branch of Shingon Esoteric Buddhism. Like the Kangaku-in, the Kanchi-in is a scholastic center. Established in the first half of the fourteenth century, it suffered extreme damage in the 1596 earthquake that destroyed much of the Tō-ji temple complex. Repairs were carried out soon thereafter through the support of the Toyotomi family, the present guest hall dating from 1605. This date is confirmed by the extant *munafuda*, which records the history of a building project and is attached to, or written directly on, the building's ridgepole. Moreover, in a rare piece of good fortune, the identity of the head carpenter is known as well, the name Fujii Iwami no Kami Yoshitsugu having been inked on the back of a gable ornament.

Characteristics of the Plan

The plan of the Kanchi-in Guest Hall is different from those of the Kōjō-in and Kangaku-in guest halls in that the southern wall, not the eastern, is the main facade (pl. 66). The entry porch (*kurumayose*) and "Chinese" gable are built into the east side of this main facade (pl. 67). The rooms of the interior are arranged in two rows, that of the south containing the Jōza no Ma (ten mats) to the east and the Tsugi no Ma (fifteen mats) to the west. The north row is comprised of the Rajō no Ma (eight mats) to the east, the Naka no Ma (six mats) at the center, and the Shisha no Ma (six mats) to the west. Broad verandas flanked by outer verandas one step lower surround the structure, the south broad veranda extending to the east to constitute a *chūmon-rō*. Interestingly, the Jōza no Ma and Tsugi no Ma do not extend perpendicular to the facade as in the Kōjō-in and Kangaku-in guest halls, but rather are parallel to it, the entry porch (*kurumayose*) leading not to the Tsugi no Ma, but directly into the Jōza no Ma. The entrance hall (*genkan*) is a later addition.

The Jōza no Ma is the audience room of the structure, and it includes on its east wall a two-bay *tokonoma* to the south and half-bay-wide shelves beside it to the north (pl. 68). The room is separated from the Tsugi no Ma by four *fusuma*, with a transom of bamboo-joint motif suspended above (pl. 69). Despite this separation of the Jōza no Ma and the Tsugi no Ma, however, the ceiling above is continuous, and is finished with thin, parallel ceiling battens extending the length of the two rooms, this style known as a *saobuchi* ceiling.

The Rajō no Ma includes a one-bay *tsukeshoin* built into the south end of the east wall and a one-and-a-half-bay *chōdaigamae* at the west serving as the entrance to the Naka no Ma (pl. 70). The absence of *tokonoma* and staggered shelves gives the room a living area quality. Although the four walls of the Naka no Ma are now mostly *fusuma*, marks on the columns suggest the room was once enclosed by fixed walls, which must have created a very confined atmosphere. The ceiling of the Naka no Ma

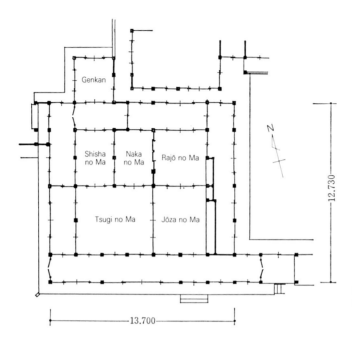

66. Plan of the Kanchi-in Guest Hall, Kyōōgokoku-ji (Tō-ji).

as well is lower than those of the flanking rooms. These two characteristics suggest that the Naka no Ma was a sleeping space (*nando*). The *chōdaigamae* thus retains here its original use as an entry from a space for daily living to a sleeping area.

Conservative and Advanced Aspects of the Kanchi-in Guest Hall
In the guest halls of Onjō-ji, emphasis was placed on public audience spaces, with areas for private residential purposes losing importance by comparison. The Kanchi-in Guest Hall, however, retains emphasis on rooms actually meant for daily use as private areas. This is definitely an early *shoin* characteristic. Furthermore, the Kanchi-in Guest Hall includes the Jōza no Ma formal room, Rajō no Ma living space, and Naka no Ma sleeping area under one roof and, moreover, locates them in close connection to one another. This trend, too, is removed from mature *shoin* such as the Ninomaru Palace, in which public and private rooms are separated and included in entirely different structures. The details of the interior are also of early nature, in that the Jōza no Ma and Tsugi no Ma are linked by a continuous batten (*saobuchi*) ceiling (pl. 69), and that there is neither *tsukeshoin* nor *chōdaigamae* in the main audience room.

The exterior of the structure retains the overall appearance of the Onjō-ji buildings, but incorporates significant changes in detail. The *chūmon-rō* here has lost its original function as an entrance/waiting area and become simply a corridor. The "Chinese" gable is retained, but the door of the entry porch (*kurumayose*) is not a swinging one as on the Onjō-ji examples, but rather one of the sliding wooden door (*mairado*) types

67. South facade of the Kanchi-in Guest Hall, Kyōōgokoku-ji (Tō-ji).

68. *Tokonoma*, staggered shelves, and *chōdaigamae* of the Jōza no Ma; Kanchi-in Guest Hall, Kyōōgokoku-ji (Tō-ji).
69. Jōza no Ma viewed from the Tsugi no Ma; Kanchi-in Guest Hall, Kyōōgokoku-ji (Tō-ji).
70. *Chōdaigamae* of the Rajō no Ma; Kanchi-in Guest Hall, Kyōōgokoku-ji (Tō-ji).

(pl. 67). *Mairado* have replaced the *shinden*-style reticulated shutters (*shitomido*) of the Onjō-ji structures as well. The uniform use of *mairado* is definitely a forward-looking aspect of the building.

The Guest Hall of the Kanchi-in thus incorporates both conservative and progressive elements, and consequently occupies a middle stage in the development of the mature *shoin* style.

The Saikyō-ji Guest Hall

Saikyō-ji is located on the east side of Mount Hiei. It is within walking distance of the great Enryaku-ji on Hiei's summit and provides a splendid view of Lake Biwa. The headquarters of the Shinzei school of Tendai Buddhism, Saikyō-ji dates to Heian times, but was razed in 1571 by Oda Nobunaga during his devastating attack on the Mount Hiei monasteries. According to a copy of the ridgepole certificate (*munafuda*), the present Guest Hall was erected at its present location in the last month of 1598. Furthermore, according to temple records, a building on the grounds of Hideyoshi's Fushimi Castle at Shigetsu was moved to Saikyō-ji in the same year. The records are, however, imprecise, and studies now available indicate that the Guest Hall was most likely originally part of Fushimi Castle itself.

Interior Configuration
The Guest Hall plan is of two rows, each one being divided basically into three spaces (pl. 71). Thus, although some of the spaces are further subdivided into smaller rooms, the building conforms in general to the standard abbot's quarters configuration of six rooms in two rows.

The main audience room of the structure is the Jōza no Ma of eighteen mats (pl. 72). It includes on its west wall a two-bay *tokonoma* to the north, and at the south veranda side one-bay-wide staggered shelves. The shelf alcove includes upper cabinets and shelves built in the tripartite *seirō-dana* style with the central section raised (pl. 73). The floorboards of both the *tokonoma* and shelf alcove are bordered with up-to-date moldings (*kamachi*), and are quite thick. Older-style elements remain, however, in that the floorboards are raised high above the *tatami* level of the room and a *kegomiita* is included. The marked thickness of the lintel and the thinness of the shelves are old designs as well, as is the locating of the shelves and not the *tokonoma* nearer to the veranda. Late Muromachi styling is seen in the high level of the wooden wainscoting of the *shōji* and in the thinness of the frieze rails.

The Enkō no Ma (eighteen mats) has a *tokonoma* at the south side of the west wall. To the north of the *tokonoma* is a pair of sliding screens leading to an entry into the small rooms in the building's northwest corner. The lintel of this *tokonoma* is thinner than that of the Jōza no Ma example. The Jōza no Ma *tokonoma* consequently appears to

101

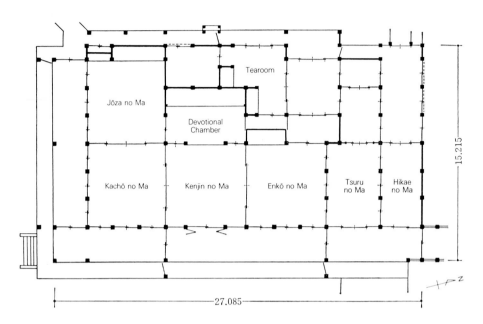

Tearoom

Jōza no Ma

Devotional
Chamber

Kachō no Ma

Kenjin no Ma

Enkō no Ma

Tsuru
no Ma

Hikae
no Ma

15.215

27.085

71. Plan of the Guest Hall, Saikyō-ji.

be of an earlier style than that of the Enkō no Ma, implying that the latter was newly built when the building was moved early in the Keichō era (1596–1615).

The other important rooms in the Guest Hall are the Kachō no Ma (eighteen mats), which functions as an anteroom to the main audience hall, and the Kenjin no Ma. The latter (eighteen mats) corresponds to the central room of an abbot's quarters, being located in front of the Butsuma and set off from the flanking rooms by transoms made in the bamboo-joint style. In abbot's quarters this room is known in general as the *shitchū*. At the Saikyō-ji temple, the position of the room is indicated on the exterior of the structure by a pair of double-folding paneled Chinese-style doors.

The plan shows an amalgamation of an abbot's quarters plan and *shoin*-style detailing, with the rooms on the south and east sides of public orientation and those to the northwest for private use (pl. 71). This arrangement, however, may not be original, the temple records shedding little light on this element of the Guest Hall history. Although the building in general shows the old abbot's quarters plan, the emphasis on public reception areas is much stronger than in the medieval abbot's quarters. This public orientation is clearly due to the influence of the *shoin* style. The interior detailing as well depends heavily on *shoin* ideas, shown most strongly in the Jōza no Ma. Although much of the detail in this room is of early date, the juxtaposition of staggered shelves and *tokonoma*, rather than shelves and *tsukeshoin*, is an advanced element.

72. *Tokonoma* and staggered shelves of the Jōza no Ma; Guest Hall, Saikyō-ji

73. Staggered shelves (detail) of the Jōza no Ma; Guest Hall, Saikyō-ji.

The Zuigan-ji Hondō

The Zuigan-ji is the most magnificent temple from the Momoyama period in all of northeastern Japan. Located in Miyagi Prefecture, it is near the coast of Matsushima Bay, an area of superb natural scenery. The temple grounds have an ancient history, having been the site of the Tendai Buddhist monastery called Empuku-ji, said to have been established in 828 by the monk Ennin (794–864), famous also for his travels in T'ang China. Ennin was the disciple of Saichō (767–822) who introduced the Tendai teachings into Japan, and who founded the Tendai monastery on Mount Hiei to the northeast of Kyoto.

In the Kamakura period the Empuku-ji was changed to a Rinzai Zen temple at the behest of the regent Hōjō Tokiyori (1227–63), and served thereafter as a major center of Rinzai Zen in northeastern Japan. By the end of the Muromachi period, however, the fortunes of the Empuku-ji had declined and its buildings had fallen into decay. But the move of the great daimyo Date Masamune (1567–1636) to the nearby city of Sendai in 1600 occasioned renewed interest in the temple, and planning for its renovation was begun in 1604. It is said that Masamune, famous not only as a warrior but as an able administrator and patron of the arts, laid out the approximate plans himself. According to temple records and to an extant ridgepole certificate, ground breaking for the Hondō took place in 1605 and the ridgepole was set in 1609. At that time the name of the temple was changed to Seiryūzan Zuigan-ji.

Characteristics of the Plan

The center of the Zuigan-ji complex is the Hondō, which faces southeast (pls. 74, 75). Though the building functions as an abbot's quarters (*hōjō*), it is known as the Hondō or "Main Hall." To the northeast are the kitchens (Kuri), connected to the Hondō by a wide corridor. Arranged side by side in front of the Hondō are the Onarimon, or Processional Gate, and the Chūmon gate, this Chūmon a free-standing structure not to be confused with the *chūmon-rō*, the entrance arcade of the *shuden*-style *shoin*. The Hondō, gates, and Kuri are linked by a wall and form an enclosed courtyard (pl. 82). This connected group of structures constitutes the core of the temple, and all were constructed at the same time.

The Hondō has a standard rectangular abbot's quarters plan, with two rows of three major spaces each. This is the plan seen in the Ryōgin-an Hōjō (pl. 17) and the Guest Hall of Saikyō-ji (pl. 71), both previously discussed. The major spaces of the Zuigan-ji Hondō are, however, further subdivided into a number of smaller rooms, and there is no left-right symmetry to the arrangement of these smaller spaces.

The main room of the Hondō is the Jōdan no Ma (eighteen mats) located in the west corner (pls. 76, 84). It includes all the major elements of a formal *shoin*-style audience chamber, with *tokonoma*, staggered shelves, *chōdaigamae*, and a *jōdan*, with a smaller space raised one step further (the *jōjōdan*) projecting to the southwest and including a *tsukeshoin* and a second set of staggered shelves (pls. 77–78). To the northeast of the Jōdan no Ma is the Butsuma (Devotional Chamber), located in the central position of the back (northwest) row of rooms. It includes an altar on its west wall. The north corner space of the Hondō is subdivided into the Rakan no Ma (twelve mats) to the southwest and the Sumie no Ma (eighteen mats) to the northeast. The room corresponding to the Sumie no Ma in a typical abbot's quarters plan is reserved for the living and study quarters of the abbot, and this room at the Zuigan-ji has an unmistakable living area quality, including staggered shelves on its southwest side and a *tsukeshoin* adjacent to them at the northwest (pl. 79).

The front (southeast) row of rooms begins with the Bunnō no Ma (thirty mats) at the south corner, directly in front of the Jōdan no Ma. The Kujaku no Ma, in front of the Butsuma at the center of the southeast row, has a wooden floor with one line of *tatami* laid at its periphery. To its northeast are the Taka no Ma (Rei no Ma; thirty mats) and, northeast of that, two smaller rooms, the Matsu no Ma (twelve mats) at the east corner and the Kiku no Ma (eight mats) behind it, at the center of the northeast facade.

The building has broad verandas on all but the rear (northwest) side, and outer verandas one step lower on all four. Because of the heavy snow in northeastern Japan, the outer verandas have been fitted here with wooden doors. Projecting from the south side of the main (east) facade is an entrance area, the Onari Genkan, built on a zigzag plan (pls. 80–81). In front of it is the Onari-mon, the Processional Gate, through which the daimyo, on formal visits, would pass, then enter the Onari Genkan, and thence proceed into the Hondō proper (pl. 75).

The Onari Genkan here replaces the older *kurumayose* and *chūmon-rō* characteristic of the earlier *shuden*-style *shoin*. It has a superb hipped-and-gabled roof with a "Chinese" gable attached at the front. Diagonally across the courtyard at the east is located a second *genkan* which serves as the entryway to the northeastern corridor. This *genkan*-corridor arrangement is the usual one for abbot's quarters, the Onari Genkan configuration being seldom used in them. This Hondō may be in fact the first example of a *genkan* attached directly to a *shoin* structure. It is an arrangement which soon hereafter becomes a standard element of mature *shoin* designs.

The northeast *genkan* leads as well to the temple kitchens (Kuri; pl. 82). Built at the same time as the Hondō, it has a massive pitched roof with its gable end facing the southeast as does the main Hondō facade. The pitched roof plus the cupolalike chimney with hipped-and-gabled roof make the Kuri very typical of Zen-style temple kitchens. The Kuri is connected to the Hondō by a wide corridor, the floor of which is raised above the ground. The east *genkan* abuts on the southeast end of this corridor (pl. 75). The corridor has a narrow border on its southwest side fitted with an ornamental rail of unique style. Both this corridor and the Kuri have, like the Hondō, been designated National Treasures.

105

74. Southeast facade of the Hondō, Zuigan-ji.

75. Plan of the Hondō and Kuri, Zuigan-ji.

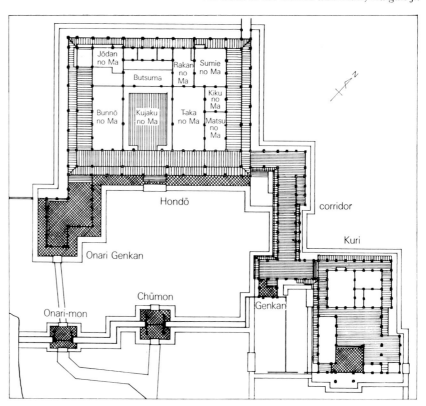

76. Jōdan no Ma of the Hondō, Zuigan-ji.

77. *Tokonoma* and *jōjōdan* of the Jōdan no Ma; Hondō, Zuigan-ji.   107

78. *Jōjōdan* of the Jōdan no Ma; Hondō, Zuigan-ji.

79. *Tsukeshoin* and staggered shelves of the Sumie no Ma; Hondō, Zuigan-ji.

80. Southeast facade of the Onari Genkan; Hondō, Zuigan-ji.

81. Interior of the Onari Genkan; Hondō, Zuigan-ji.

82. Southeast facades of the Kuri
(right) and Hondō (background, left),
Zuigan-ji.

The Hondō Jōdan no Ma

The appointments of the Jōdan no Ma are of surpassing magnificence, befitting the station of the daimyo Masamune, lord of one of the largest domains in Momoyama Japan. On the main (northwest) wall of the room are installed a two-bay *tokonoma* at the southwest and staggered shelves one bay wide at the northeast (pl. 84). The floorboards of both *tokonoma* and shelf alcove (pl. 85) have thick moldings (*kamachi*), and the shelves of the latter are thick as well, this being a characteristic of mature *shoin* styles. A two-bay *chōdaigamae* is built into the northeast wall (pl. 86). Because the Butsuma, and not a sleeping and storage space, is located behind these doors, however, they do not open and are thus purely decorative. The ten *tatami* mats nearest the *tokonoma*, shelves, and *chōdaigamae* are raised one step above the other eight *tatami* in the room and constitute a *jōdan* (the name of the room deriving from this elevated floor area).

At the southwest side of the northwest wall, the six-mat *jōjōdan* projects into the southwest broad veranda (pl. 83). It incorporates at its northwest side a shelf alcove one bay wide (pl. 88) and, at its southwest side, a one-and-a-half-bay *tsukeshoin* (pl. 87).

83. *Jōjōdan* of the Jōdan no Ma;
Hondō, Zuigan-ji.

The Jōdan no Ma plan, then, has a configuration nearly identical to that of the "*shuden* plan" in the Heinouchi family's *Shōmei* building guide (pl. 55). The only differences are that the section projecting into the broad veranda is here a *jōjōdan* and not simply a *jōdan*, and that it includes shelves and not a subsidiary *tokonoma*. Interestingly, records show that the lumber for the building was ordered from Mount Kumano in the Kii domains (present-day Wakayama Prefecture), several weeks' journey on foot to the south. The carpenter Gyōbuzaimon Kunitsugu, from the same region, was called in to draw up the plans. That the Heinouchi family also came originally from Kii suggests that the close relationship between the Jōdan no Ma and *Shōmei* design may not have been coincidental.

But whereas the "*shuden* plan" and the related Kōjō-in *shuden*-style Guest Hall (pl. 54) are representative of the early *shoin* style, the Zuigan-ji Jōdan no Ma is conceived in far greater magnificence and is on the verge of exhibiting the completely mature audience hall *shoin* style. The proportions of the *tokonoma*, shelf alcove, and *chōdaigamae* reflect mature *shoin* designs. A *jōdan* and a *jōjōdan* are included, and the ceiling above is coved and coffered as befits an audience hall for a great lord. The screen paintings are dazzling creations of gold and polychrome and are bordered by frieze rails with gold fittings. The transom over the *tsukeshoin* is intricately carved (pl. 87), as are the transoms of the other rooms. Thus the Hondō of the Zuigan-ji prefigures the mature *shoin* magnificence of the Edo period.

Confluence of the Abbot's Quarters and the Shoin Style

The Zuigan-ji Hondō is one of the most representative *shoin*-style abbot's quarters remaining from the Momoyama period, and it well reflects the gradual change that the Zen abbot's quarters had undergone since its beginnings in the middle ages. As will be recalled from Chapter Two, the abbot's quarters came into being as the living area of the abbot in a Zen monastery. By the time the Zuigan-ji was constructed, however, the abbot's quarters had taken on important public functions as well, being used more and more frequently for the meeting and entertainment of visitors. The Zuigan-ji was designed from the outset with the public function in mind and incorporates all the magnificent detail necessary for the reception of its patron, Lord Date Masamune.

This necessary detail is adopted from contemporary *shoin* designs. As was earlier pointed out, although the *shoin* style had its roots in the living quarters of Muromachi monks, there are no extant abbot's quarters from that period incorporating the "furniture" of *shoin* interiors, the *tokonoma*, staggered shelves, *tsukeshoin*, and *chōdaigamae*. By the Momoyama period, however, most abbot's quarters included, as the Zuigan-ji eloquently shows, some or all of these *shoin* interior elements. Thus by the late sixteenth century influences had reversed themselves, with mature *shoin*-style elements being adopted back into the monastic structure out of which the *shoin* style had first begun to develop.

The Zuigan-ji is a particularly valuable example of a Momoyama *shoin*-style abbot's quarters. Not only were detailed records made and preserved concerning the construction, but it remains today essentially in its original configuration. This is as opposed to many other extant Momoyama structures which underwent later additions and renovations in styles varying from the original.

84. Jōdan no Ma of the Hondō, Zuigan-ji.
Although the Zuigan-ji is located in northeastern Japan, far from Kyoto, the cultural center of the country, it is in no way inferior in design or elegance to Kyoto structures. The Jōdan no Ma, in fact, is the most magnificent of extant *shoin* of the Momoyama period. Its plan is very like that of the "*shuden* plan" in the *Shōmei* and the Kōjō-in Guest Hall, but the decoration is far more lavish.

85 (following page). Staggered shelves of the Jōdan no Ma; Hondō, Zuigan-ji.
The shelf alcove of the Jōdan no Ma proper is narrower than that of the *jōjōdan* area, and the older arrangement of two staggered shelves, rather than three, has been used accordingly. When used in tandem with a *tokonoma* space, this type of shelf gives a sense of balance and formality. The metalwork and the polychrome paintings are done in the same style as those of the *jōjōdan* shelves, and the upper cabinets are likewise painted with heavenly maidens. The shelves and the *tokonoma* are both quite shallow. A comparison of these shelves with those of the Tōgu-dō Dōjin-sai shows not only much more decoration here but thicker wooden members as well.

86 (opposite page, top). *Chōdaigamae* of the Jōdan no Ma; Hondō, Zuigan-ji.

In the Zuigan-ji Jōdan no Ma, the *chōdaigamae* doors no longer lead into a subsidiary space but are instead solely for decorative purposes. The Jōdan no Ma, however, was designed for the visits of a great daimyo, and to compensate for the nonfunctioning *chōdaigamae*, the *tokonoma* was fitted with *fusuma* behind an ogee-arch motif to serve as an emergency entrance for bodyguards (pl. 84).

85. See preceding page for caption.

87. *Tsukeshoin* of the Jōdan no Ma *jōjōdan*; Hondō, Zuigan-ji.

The *tsukeshoin* of the Jōdan no Ma is of archetypical design, with a writing surface one step above the level of the *jōdan* floor and four wainscoted *shōji* with a transom above. The *shōji* have a very fine latticework and gold clasps, and the wainscoting beneath is embellished with paintings of green bamboo against a gold ground. The transom incorporates an intricate diamond lattice. The overall effect is one of marked beauty and unity. Although the configuration of the alcove is of an old style, the details of the decoration are clearly up-to-date.

115

88. Staggered shelves of the Jōdan no Ma *jōjō-dan*; Hondō, Zuigan-ji.

The *jōjōdan* of the Zuigan-ji Jōdan no Ma incorporates a *tsukeshoin* and staggered shelves. In this it is even closer to the "*shuden* plan" in the *Shōmei* than the Kōjō-in Guest Hall, which substitutes for shelves a *tokonoma*. Although the *tsukeshoin*-shelf juxtaposition recalls the study areas of Muromachi structures, this *jōjōdan* was most likely a relaxation area or a place for changing robes. The shelves are built in the tripartite *seirō-dana* style, with the added innovation that the lower flanking shelves vary in height. The retaining molding of the uppermost shelf, gold appointments, and polychrome and gold paintings are evocative of the late Momoyama style.

4

THE EDO-PERIOD SHOIN

The *shoin* reaches its mature phase early in the seventeenth century. It was at this time that Tokugawa Ieyasu (1542–1616) achieved ultimate power in the land and established the Tokugawa shogunate which was to survive for the following two and a half centuries. In the manner of the first Kamakura shogun, Minamoto no Yoritomo, Ieyasu located his government far from Kyoto and the Throne, and his castle in Edo soon became the center of a mammoth city, eventually the largest on earth at that time. To weaken the power of the rival lords, especially that of the *tozama* daimyo who had accepted Tokugawa hegemony only after the battle of Seki-gahara, the shogunate demanded they alternate their residences regularly between their own fiefs and Edo, and, furthermore, leave their wives and children permanently in the city. This system of "alternate attendance" (*sankin kōtai*) required the approximately 270 daimyo to build expensive Edo residences and staff them handsomely, thus depleting their coffers but causing an increase in the construction by the upper-class military of ornate Edo mansions in the latest style, the *shoin* style.

Ieyasu's son, Hidetada (1579–1632), became shogun in 1605 on his father's ostensible retirement, and was in turn succeeded by his son Iemitsu (1604–51) in 1623. They were as anxious as their forebear to cement Tokugawa power, and they relentlessly curtailed all perceived as detrimental to that end, most notably Christianity and European influence. The resultant policy of exclusion and seclusion cut Japan nearly completely off from the rest of the world until 1854, when two ports were opened to Commodore Matthew C. Perry. The architecture of the Tokugawa castles and palaces served this design of subjugation as well, the richly appointed interiors of these residences reflecting the supreme dominance of those ruling within. The other lords, too, adopted the style according to the capacity of their treasuries, not only in their Edo mansions but in their home fiefs as well, where they continued to possess considerable military strength and administrative autonomy.

It has recently become clear that two of the structures which epitomize the high-style *shoin* do not date from the Momoyama period as traditionally thought, but rather from the early Edo period, specifically the Kan'ei era (1624–44). The Nino-maru Palace of Nijō Castle, once thought to have been moved from Hideyoshi's

Juraku-dai castle-palace (completed in 1587), is now believed to date almost certainly to 1626. The Shoin of Nishi Hongan-ji was believed as well to have been part of one of Hideyoshi's Momoyama-period Fushimi Castle structures. It has, however, been recently shown that it was most probably built from the first at its present location in 1632–33. Our conception of typical Momoyama architecture must be reconsidered in light of these discoveries.

Chapter Four will focus on the most important *shoin*-style warrior residences and temple structures of the Edo period, giving special attention to the quintessential *shoin* building, the Ninomaru Palace. Although it was in the Edo period as well that the fusion of the *shoin* and teahouse styles occurred in the *sukiya shoin*, discussion of that development is postponed until Chapter Five.

Ninomaru Palace of Nijō Castle

The Ninomaru Palace is the finest example of a mature *shoin* building still in existence. The Nijō Castle of which it forms a part was built to serve as the residence of Ieyasu when affairs of state brought him to Kyoto, and was by and large completed in 1606. It was enlarged during Hidetada's administration in 1619. The Ninomaru Palace is thought to have been begun in 1624 by Iemitsu, in preparation for the visit in 1626 of Emperor Gomizunoo, builder of Shugaku-in Detached Palace. There are no written records unquestionably proving the 1624–26 construction project to have been that of the Ninomaru Palace. In light, however, of both the oblique references to it in various documents of the 1620s and the close correlation of the architectural style to that of other definitively dated buildings of that decade, it is highly likely that the 1624–26 project was indeed that of the Ninomaru.

With the destruction during World War Two of Nagoya Castle and its palace, the Ninomaru Palace assumed a unique position among mature *shoin*-style structures. Only one other palace built within a castle remains beside it, the Kaitoku-kan of Kōchi Castle. The present Kaitoku-kan is, however, a version rebuilt in later years. It will be discussed at the end of this chapter.

Characteristics of the Plan

The Ninomaru Palace occupies the southeast corner of the castle complex. To the west is the Hommaru main compound which is surrounded by massive stone walls and a wide moat. The five-story donjon which originally towered above the surrounding buildings was destroyed by lightning in 1750. To reach the palace, one enters the castle at the Higashi Ōtemon gate, follows the earthen wall first south and then west, then turns north and passes under the "Chinese" Gate (Karamon) set into the wall's south side (pl. 1). Across the courtyard is the palace entrance, the Kurumayose, with the palace buildings extending diagonally from it to the north-

west (pl. 89). Behind this main palace complex is a secondary building, once connected but now separate, in which food was prepared. A large landscape garden is situated at the southwest (pl. 91). Though both the Nijō Castle as a whole and the Ninomaru Palace within it used to be more extensive than they are today, the most important series of Ninomaru structures remain, and these quite adequately represent the grandeur of the original conception.

The Kurumayose is roofed in the hipped-and-gabled style and incorporates a curved "Chinese" gable as well (pl. 90). No longer a simple entry porch as on the Kōjō-in Guest Hall, the Kurumayose here is an entire entry structure. Directly behind the Kurumayose is the Tōzamurai, in area the largest building in the Ninomaru complex. Its southern gable towers above the Kurumayose, the golden ornament giving the visitor a taste of what is to come in the interior.

West of the Tōzamurai is the Shikidai (a reception building), and, west of that, the Ōhiroma, the central and most important building in the palace complex. Like the Tōzamurai, the Ōhiroma is roofed in the hipped-and-gabled style, with gables facing north and south (pl. 1). These three buildings are all contiguous and constitute the public half of the palace.

The more private areas are reached through a corridor exiting from the northwest corner of the Ōhiroma (pl. 89). This corridor was originally covered with fifty-four *tatami* mats and is known as the Sotetsu no Ma or "Palm Room" by virtue of the subjects painted on its screens. It leads to the Kuroshoin building, the south wall of which borders on the landscape garden (pl. 91). The Kuroshoin is in turn connected to the Shiroshoin by another corridor running flush with the west side of the two buildings. The Kuroshoin and Shiroshoin are both roofed in the hipped-and-gabled style.

The Constituent Buildings

The entrance building of the complex, the Tōzamurai, served as the palace waiting area. It was also used as a guard post by retainers, the incorporation of a *tōzamurai* having a long tradition in warrior residences. The Tōzamurai itself includes three rows of rooms, with the major room, the Chokushi no Ma, located in the northeast corner. The Chokushi no Ma is divided into two levels, the *jōdan* (twenty-one mats) at the east and the *gedan* (thirty-five mats) at the west. The main wall of the *jōdan* exhibits a *tokonoma* and staggered shelves and the south wall incorporates a *chōdaigamae* (pl. 92).

The Shikidai, west of the Tōzamurai, is a reception area composed of two rows of rooms. The next building, the Ōhiroma, is the central structure of the complex. Though slightly smaller than the Tōzamurai, it too is of a three-row plan (pl. 8). The main audience hall of the building, also called the Ōhiroma, was used for formal audiences, as pointed out in the Introduction.

In 1587, well before the Ninomaru Palace was built, an Ōhiroma complex was built at Hideyoshi's Juraku-dai castle-palace. The name, literally "greater [ō] large [hiro] space [ma],"* was derived from its dimensions, which were much greater than

---

* *Hiroma* is the generic term, the ō prefix appearing in some examples and not in others.

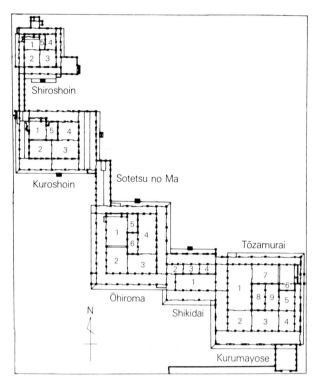

89. Plan of the main complex, Ninomaru Palace, Nijō Castle.

Tōzamurai—1) Tora no Ma Ichi no Ma (59½ mats), 2) Tora no Ma Ni no Ma (28 mats), 3) Tora no Ma San no Ma (40 mats), 4) Yanagi no Ma (18 mats), 5) Wakamatsu no Ma (24 mats), 6) Chōdai no Ma, 7) Chokushi no Ma (56 mats), 8) storage, 9) Fuyō no Ma. Shikidai—1) Shikidai no Ma (24 mats), 2) Rōjū Ichi no Ma (14 mats), 3) Rōjū Ni no Ma (24 mats), 4) Rōjū San no Ma (24 mats). Ōhiroma—1) Jōdan no Ma (Ichi no Ma; 48 mats), 2) Gedan no Ma (Ni no Ma; 44 mats), 3) San no Ma (44 mats), 4) Yon no Ma (52½ mats), 5) Chōdai no Ma, 6) storage space. Kuroshoin—1) Jōdan no Ma (Ichi no Ma; 24 mats), 2) Ni no Ma (31½ mats), 3) San no Ma (35 mats), 4) Yon no Ma (28 mats), 5) Chōdai no Ma (13 mats). Shiroshoin—1) Jōdan no Ma (Ichi no Ma or Shiroshoin; 15 mats), 2) Ni no Ma (18 mats), 3) San no Ma (18 mats), 4) Yon no Ma (12 mats), 5) Chōdai no Ma.

those of the standard *shuden* being built at that time (see Chapter Three). The main room in the Ōhiroma complex served as the main audience chamber of the palace. A plan generally resembling that of the Juraku-dai Ōhiroma is also found in the Heinouchi *Shōmei* of 1608 (pl. 63). Because this plan is entitled "Plan of a Contemporary Hiroma," it appears that "contemporary" here roughly indicates the time period from 1608, the year the book was written, back to the Tenshō era (1573–92) in which Hideyoshi's Ōhiroma was built. As pointed out in Chapter Three, a comparison of this *hiroma* plan labeled "contemporary" with the *shuden* plan labeled "old" in the 1608 *Shōmei* (pl. 55) indicates that in general the transition from *shuden* to *hiroma* occurred in the late sixteenth and early seventeenth centuries, though considerable overlap of styles is seen at that time.

This *Shōmei* three-row *hiroma* plan is reflected quite closely in the Ninomaru Tōzamurai and, with variation, in the Ōhiroma of the palace. A major difference between this multirow conception and that of the *shuden* is the fact that the Ninomaru Ōhiroma is basically designed with only the public-formal function in mind. The more private activities generally carried out in the back row of the *shuden* building are here consigned to entirely separate structures, the Kuroshoin and the Shiroshoin.

90. Kurumayose of the Ninomaru Palace, Nijō Castle.

The Kuroshoin was used for more private interviews and for daily affairs of state. That the Kuroshoin is not contiguous to the Ōhiroma, but connected at a distance, emphasizes its private nature, as does its location in the rear half of the complex. It is smaller in size than the Ōhiroma, with only two rows of rooms. Consequently, it was originally known in contradistinction as the "Kohiroma" or "Small Hiroma," the name Kuroshoin (Black Shoin) being a later development.

Appropriate to its status as the main room in the Kuroshoin, the Jōdan no Ma includes a *tokonoma* of two and a half bays on its north wall and a one-bay shelf alcove beside it at the east (pls. 94, 101). In a variation on the standard scheme, however, a second shelf alcove is located on the east wall, at right angles to that of the main wall. South of the second shelf alcove is a *chōdaigamae* of two and a half bays which opens into the adjacent Chōdai no Ma. A *tsukeshoin* projects into the west veranda. Although the overall scale of the combined Jōdan no Ma and Ni no Ma is smaller than the audience area of the Ōhiroma complex, the Ni no Ma (*gedan*) portion (thirty-one-and-a-half mats) is here larger than the *jōdan* (twenty-four mats) to make the space convenient for large audiences. The cherry tree wall paintings are of smaller scale than the pines of the Ōhiroma and are more approachable and less awe-inspiring.

121

91. Ninomaru Palace viewed from the west
across the landscape garden; Nijō Castle.

92. *Chōdaigamae* of the Chokushi no Ma *jōdan*; Tōzamurai of the Ninomaru
Palace, Nijō Castle.

93. Jōdan no Ma and Ni no Ma viewed from the San no Ma; Kuroshoin, Nijō Castle.

94. Jōdan no Ma viewed from the Ni no Ma; Kuroshoin of the Ninomaru Palace, Nijō Castle.

The personal living quarters of the shogun were located in the Shiroshoin, also called the Goza no Ma or Gyoza no Ma, connected by a second corridor to the Kuro-shoin at the south. Its plan is roughly divided into quadrants, the main Jōdan no Ma (fifteen mats; also called the Ichi no Ma or Shiroshoin) being located again in the northwest (pl. 89). The Ni no Ma (eighteen mats) borders it on the south. The east quadrant is comprised of the Chōdai no Ma and, in the northeast corner, the Yon no Ma (twelve mats). The San no Ma (eighteen mats) in the southeast corner completes the plan.

Here again, the Jōdan no Ma has a *tokonoma* (two bays) and staggered shelves (one bay) located west and east on the main (north) wall (pl. 95). On the west wall is a one-and-a-half-bay *tsukeshoin*, and on the east is a two-and-a-half-bay *chōdaigamae*, behind which is the Chōdai no Ma. Because of the very personal nature of this building, the Jōdan no Ma and Ni no Ma spaces can be partitioned off with sliding screens. Appropriate as well to a room designed for rest and relaxation rather than for ceremony and intimidation are the simple staggered shelves and wall paintings of quiet scenes in subdued color.

The Ninomaru Palace and the Mature Shoin Style

The Ninomaru Palace is the quintessential extant example of a *shoin* complex. The main room of each of its constituent buildings uniformly follows a set design prescription, with the main wall incorporating a *tokonoma* on the veranda side and staggered shelves on the side bordering the interior rooms of the building. A *chōdaigamae* flanks the shelves and leads to an interior room. All rooms save the Chokushi no Ma of the Tōzamurai have a *tsukeshoin* across from the *chōdaigamae*, projecting into the veranda. The main wall, furthermore, is located at the back of the *jōdan*, which is raised one level above the floors of the surrounding rooms.

Furthermore, each building in the complex has its own single, clearly defined purpose. This separation by function is opposed to the typical *shinden*-style arrangement which incorporates public and private functions within a single large space. The building names used in mature *shoin* complexes—*ōhiroma* for the main formal audience space and *kohiroma* for the smaller and less formal audience space—are known in later structures as the *ōjoin* ("great *shoin*") and the *koshoin* ("small *shoin*"), the progression from *ōjoin* to *koshoin* to private *goza no ma* becoming standard for daimyo residences. It is at this point that the term *shoin* comes to indicate an entire structure rather than simply a room therein. The formularization of the interior scheme, the separation of buildings according to function, and the application of the term *shoin* to whole buildings mark the maturity of the *shoin* style.

THE SHOIN OF NISHI HONGAN-JI

The Nishi Hongan-ji temple is the headquarters of the Hongan-ji sect of Jōdo Shinshū

95. Jōdan no Ma of the Shiroshoin; Ninomaru
Palace, Nijō Castle.

(True Pure Land) Buddhism. Jōdo Shinshū was founded by the great priest Shinran (1173–1262), a disciple of Hōnen (1133–1212), founder of Jōdo Pure Land Buddhism. It rose to major importance under its eighth patriarch Rennyo (1415–99), and its followers for the next century and more fomented frequent revolts known as *ikkō ikki* or "single-minded uprisings." Ikkō was another name for the Jōdo Shinshū sect, derived from its adherents' intense "single-minded" faith in the Amida Buddha. The Ikkō sect had considerable military strength, as seen by their defeat of the Lord of Kaga in 1470 and their personal control of the Kaga domains for the next century. They also warred for a decade with Oda Nobunaga from their fortress of Ishiyama Hongan-ji in Osaka, the great Lord Nobunaga never successfully storming that stronghold.

When first built, on land granted the Jōdo Shinshū sect by Toyotomi Hideyoshi in 1591, Nishi Hongan-ji was simply called Hongan-ji. When the Tokugawa shogunate came to power, however, it ordered the Shinshū sect to divide so as to preclude future military activity. The offshoot of the sect took the name Ōtani, and built its headquarters in 1602 to the east of the older temple. This new temple came to be known thereafter as Higashi (East) Hongan-ji, and the older one in contradistinction as Nishi (West) Hongan-ji. Nishi Hongan-ji was destroyed by an accidental fire in 1617, but rebuilding was begun soon after.

The Shinshū sect thus possessed considerable temporal power. Its doctrine as well is comparatively "this worldly," its monks keeping no fast and being encouraged to marry. These factors no doubt contributed to the opulent style adopted for the Nishi Hongan-ji buildings. The Shoin, North Nō Stage, "Chinese" Gate (Karamon), Hiun-kaku Pavilion, and the Kuroshoin are all National Treasures. The latter two are dealt with in Chapter Five.

The Shoin

Located at the south of the temple grounds, the Shoin is comprised of two major spaces, the Audience Hall, with three smaller subsidiary rooms, and the Shiroshoin (pls. 96–97). The massive 162-mat Audience Hall incorporates a *jōdan* (37 mats) and, to the east, a *jōjōdan* (5 mats; pls. 98–99). On the main wall are, from west to east, a three-bay *chōdaigamae*, three-bay *tokonoma*, and a one-bay shelf alcove, though the last is on the *jōjōdan* east wall, adjacent to the shelf alcove (pl. 100). A fan-shaped (*gumbai-gata*) window separates the *jōjōdan* space from the expanse of room to the south.

The *jōdan* space is used by the abbot, his successor apparent, and his family. The other monks assemble on the lower *gedan* to the south. The *jōjōdan*, retaining the older configuration of a study area in its incorporation of *tsukeshoin* and shelves, was perhaps used for rest and relaxation, or as a waiting area for a highly placed guest.

Although the *jōjōdan* arrangement and the incorporation of not one but two *genkan* entryways at the south is unique to the Nishi Hongan-ji, the Ōtsu Betsu-in in Ōtsu City, Shiga Prefecture, and the Daitsū-ji in the same city (discussed in the following section) show the same general audience hall arrangement, though on a somewhat smaller scale.

Tradition has it that the Shoin was originally part of Toyotomi Hideyoshi's Fushimi Castle and that its magnificence typified the style of the Momoyama period (1568–1614). In light of recent research and repairs, however, it is now believed to have been constructed from the first at its present location, in 1632, the middle of the Kan'ei era (1624–44).

To the north of the Audience Hall is the Shiroshoin. Its plan is of two rows (pl. 97), the northern including, from the east, the Shimei no Ma (twenty-four mats), the Ni no Ma (eighteen mats), and the San no Ma (eighteen mats), and the southern containing, again from the east, two subsidiary rooms (*nando*) and the Kiku no Ma (thirty mats). The Shimei no Ma is the main room of the Shiroshoin and is designed in a mature *shoin* style with a coved and coffered ceiling. The elegance of its design and its floor-to-ceiling polychromy make this room one of the most magnificent of *shoin*-style structures extant. The eastern ten mats constitute a *jōdan* area, on the main wall of which are built a two-bay *tokonoma* and, to the south, one-bay staggered shelves (pl. 102). Behind this wall is the Shōzoku no Ma (six mats), with its own *tokonoma* and staggered shelves. On the north wall of the Shimei no Ma is a *tsukeshoin*, one and a half bays wide, which projects into the northern veranda. Opposite it to the south

126

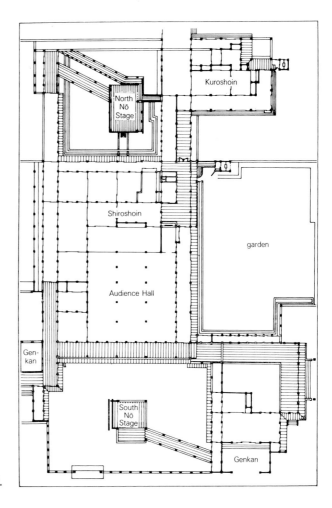

96. Plan of the Shoin, Nishi Hongan-ji.

are *chōdaigamae* doors two bays in width. Some scholars believe that the Audience Hall and the Shiroshoin were originally two separate structures, later joined to form the present configuration.

Nō Stages

The Nō drama, with its restrained pace and metaphysical import, continued in the Edo period to be a major entertainment of the warrior class. One could provide for one's guest no higher entertainment than an evening of Nō drama, and many mansions included Nō stages for this purpose. The Nishi Hongan-ji includes two exterior Nō stages and an interior one as well.

The North Nō Stage, behind the Shiroshoin, was built in 1581 and donated to Nishi Hongan-ji sometime during the Genna era (1615–24). It is the oldest Nō stage to which an exact date can be affixed (pl. 103). The roof is of the hipped-and-gabled style at the side facing the viewer, and is pitched at the back. The stage is typical of the Momoyama style, with side stage and rear stage sections located under the eaves, and a causeway under a very simple pitched roof. It has been designated a National Treasure.

97. Plan of the Audience Hall and Shiroshoin,
Nishi Hongan-ji.

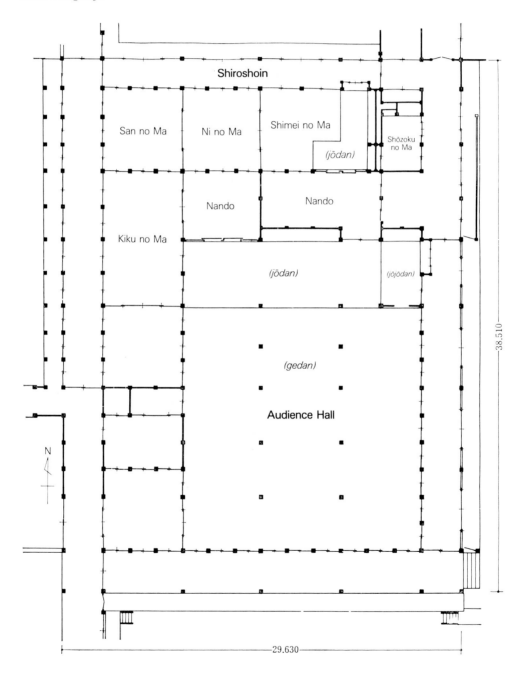

Shiroshoin

San no Ma

Ni no Ma

Shimei no Ma

(jōdan)

Shōzoku no Ma

Nando

Nando

Kiku no Ma

(jōdan)

(jōjōdan)

(gedan)

Audience Hall

N

38.510

29.630

98. Audience Hall of the Shoin, Nishi Hongan-ji.

99. *Jōjōdan* of the Audience Hall; Shoin, Nishi Hongan-ji.   129

100. *Jōdan* and *jōjōdan* of the Audience Hall, Nishi Hongan-ji.

Though expansive in their own right, the *jōdan* and *jōjōdan* of the Nishi Hongan-ji Audience Hall account for only one quarter of the entire vast space. The hall is, in fact, the largest single *shoin* space still in existence, and the rectangular *jōdan* is unique as well. The elaborate wall paintings depict classical Chinese subjects. The hall is also known as the Kō no Ma, or Room of the Great Birds, this name deriving from the splendid transom carvings.

130

101. Jōdan no Ma of the Kuroshoin; Ninomaru Palace, Nijō Castle.

The Jōdan no Ma of the Kuroshoin has the same basic style as that of the Ōhiroma, with the exception that the shelf arrangement is more complex. Here, a second shelf alcove has been added on the *chōdaigamae* wall at right angles to the shelf alcove next to the *tokonoma*. Moreover, both shelf spaces show an imaginative shelf arrangement of a more complex nature than the tripartite *seirō-dana* variety.

131

102. *Jōdan* of the Shimei no Ma; Shiroshoin, Nishi
Hongan-ji.

The South Nō Stage, moved to its present location in 1897, is an Important Cultural
Property. It also reflects the Momoyama style, but its front roof facade is pitched, not
hipped and gabled, and is decorated by a large "frog's-leg" strut which is in the shape
of an inverted "U." The floor of the interior Nō stage is located under removable
tatami mats in the south section of the Audience Hall.

Karamon
The "Chinese" Gate (Karamon) is at the south of the Nishi Hongan-ji compound
(pl. 104). As was the case with the Shoin, the gate is popularly said to come from
Fushimi Castle. Stylistic analysis indicates, though, that it was probably newly built
at about the time of the Shoin construction, in 1632–33. This gate is designed in
the *mukai-karamon* style, in which the front and back have bow-shaped "Chinese"
gables, as opposed to the style of the Sambō-in Karamon mentioned earlier, which
shows a *hira-karamon* design, in which not the front and back but rather both sides
carry the gables (pl. 40). The appointments of the gate are magnificent, with intricate carving, polychromy, and gold fixtures. Though other *karamon* that have been
designated National Treasures exist at Daitoku-ji, Hōkoku Shrine, and Hōgon-ji in
Shiga Prefecture, this is the most opulent and the most stylized. Thus the Nishi Hongan-ji is the equal of contemporary warrior palaces in not only its magnificent Shoin,
132 but its incorporation of an ornate entrance and several Nō stages.

103. North Nō Stage of the Shoin, Nishi Hongan-ji.

104. "Chinese" Gate of the Shoin, Nishi Hongan-ji.

THE DAITSŪ-JI

The Daitsū-ji, also known as the Nagahama Gobō, is a branch of Higashi Hongan-ji, the headquarters of the Ōtani branch of Jōdo Shinshū which was established by the division of the Hongan-ji temple into East and West branches in 1602. The Daitsū-ji has a very complex provenance, but seems to have first been built in 1596 on the grounds of the former Nagahama Castle as a place for adherents of Jōdo Shinshū Buddhism to assemble. In 1606 it was moved to its present location, the grounds of which were enlarged, it is thought, in 1649. Legend has it that the Hiroma and the Hondō of the Daitsū-ji were originally part of the Fushimi Castle, were later moved to Higashi Hongan-ji when that temple was established, and then moved a second time in 1652 to their present location in the Daitsū-ji compound. Doubt was thrown on this theory, however, in 1952 when, during repairs, the name of a local carpenter was discovered on the upper end of the left *tokonoma* post (*tokobashira*), which implies that the building does not have its origins in Fushimi to the south. It is more likely that the Hiroma was built from the first at its present location, at the same time as the Hondō.

The Daitsū-ji complex includes four buildings classed as Important Cultural Properties—the Hondō and Hiroma, located side by side and facing south, and the two guest halls, the Ganzan-ken and the Ran-tei, both located to the northwest of the Hiroma (pl. 106). This composition of Hondō, Hiroma, and guest apartments is also seen at Nishi Hongan-ji and represents a standard Jōdo Shinshū design.

The Hiroma

The Hiroma is comprised of a single vast 144-mat space surrounded by verandas. A *genkan* projects to the south from the building's southeast corner (pl. 106). The north thirty-six mats of the main space are raised one step as a *jōdan*, with a *tsukeshoin* (one bay), shelf alcove (one bay), *tokonoma* (three bays), and *chōdaigamae* (two bays) arranged west to east on the main wall (pls. 105, 107). This single-line composition

134

105. Hiroma, Daitsū-ji.
The Hiroma of Daitsū-ji is of the same basic
style as the Audience Hall of Nishi Hongan-ji,
having a very large rectangular *jōdan* area and
decorated wall behind. It is smaller and simpler,
however, and locates the *tsukeshoin* on the main
wall instead of in a *jōjōdan*, where it is found in
the Nishi Hongan-ji. The *tsukeshoin*, *tokonoma*,
and staggered shelves are splendidly accoutered,
but all are, nevertheless, simpler than those of
Nishi Hongan-ji. The transom, too, designed in
the grill transom style, is much less elaborate,
perhaps even too unprepossessing for as grand
a space as this.

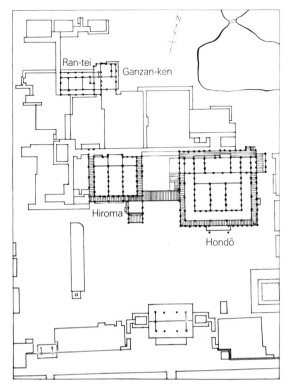

106. Plan of Daitsū-ji.

of the main *shoin* interior elements is found as well in the Nishi Hongan-ji temple and constitutes a unique Hongan-ji style. It does, however, differ from the Nishi Hongan-ji example in that it has no *jōjōdan* and that its *tsukeshoin* is on the main wall rather than at the side.

The Guest Halls

The location of the Daitsū-ji guest halls roughly corresponds to that of the Kuroshoin of Nishi Hongan-ji, being behind the main audience space, in this case to the northwest (pl. 106). The Ganzan-ken is to the east and the Ran-tei to the west, with a tearoom and an altar room between.

The Ganzan-ken is older than the Ran-tei, but its date of construction is uncertain. Its major rooms are the Ichi no Ma (ten mats) and the Ni no Ma (fifteen mats). On the west wall of the Ichi no Ma is a *tokonoma* (one bay) and on the north is a *tsukeshoin* of the same width (pl. 108). *Tsuchibisashi* eaves (also called *dobisashi*), which cover not only the building's veranda but also a few feet of ground beyond them, border the east and north sides. West of the Ganzan-ken is attached the tearoom, used most likely as a living area or a private meeting room. The garden view from the Ichi no Ma is impressive, with a distant mountain, Ibukiyama, fitting into the garden design in the "borrowed scenery" (*shakkei*) technique.

The Ran-tei dates from 1755 according to a ridgepole certificate discovered during repairs. The building is composed of one row of rooms, from east to west the Ichi no Ma (eleven mats), the Ni no Ma (fifteen mats), and the Ai no Ma (seven-and-a-half mats). Only the Ichi no Ma includes a *tokonoma* (pl. 109), and the general conception of the structure is simple and residential. In this it gives us a look at what later Japanese domestic architecture was to become.

136

107. *Tsukeshoin* and staggered shelves of the Hiroma, Daitsū-ji.

108. *Tokonoma* and *tsukeshoin* of
the Ganzan-ken, Daitsū-ji.

109. *Tokonoma* of the Ran-tei, Daitsū-ji.

The Guest Hall of Shōjū Raigō-ji

The Guest Hall of Shōjū Raigō-ji (alternately Shōju Raigō-ji) is a fine example of a mature *shoin* building decorated in a straightforward and prescribed style. The temple itself is of the Tendai sect, and has a very ancient history, having been established, it is said, by Saichō (767–822), the founder of Japanese Tendai Buddhism. In the seventeenth century it was designated a *chokugan-ji* temple by the emperor, who charged it with the offering of prayers for the welfare of the country and of himself. The Guest Hall was built, according to temple records, in 1642 as a structure for the ordination of priests and ritual transmission of the secret doctrines of the Tendai sect.

The Plan

The Guest Hall takes the plan of a standard six-room abbot's quarters of the type previously seen at Saikyō-ji in the same locale (pls. 71, 110). It varies from the Saikyō-ji plan, however, in that two extra rooms are here added to the north side of the structure, known as the "Old Shoin" (not shown in floor plan). Furthermore, because the Guest Hall serves as an ordination area, it is fitted with a special wooden floored and fixed-walled Kanjō no Ma (Ordination Room) in the northwest corner, in place of the living area traditionally found in this corner of an abbot's quarters.

The central room of the rear row, the Naijin (Inner Sanctuary), shows the characteristic wooden flooring of an abbot's quarters. To the north is the aforementioned

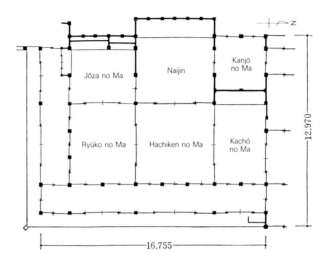

110. Plan of the Guest Hall, Shōjū Raigō-ji.

Kanjō no Ma and in front of it to the east is the Hachiken no Ma (eighteen mats). North of the Hachiken no Ma is the Kachō no Ma (twelve mats), which incorporates a two-bay *tokonoma* on its west wall, and south of it is the Ryūko no Ma (or Ryōko no Ma; fifteen mats) which serves as the anteroom to the Jōza no Ma. The Jōza no Ma (ten mats) is furnished with a *tokonoma*, staggered shelves, and *tsukeshoin*. Stylistically, the Jōza no Ma is the most important room in the complex.

The Old Shoin to the north of the six-room main section of the Guest Hall is comprised of two rooms, the eastern (nine mats) having a closet in its northwest corner, and the western (eight mats) including another closet, a *tokonoma*, and staggered shelves. The style of these two rooms appears to be of a slightly earlier period than that of the Guest Hall proper, implying that the Old Shoin was originally a separate structure.

The Jōza no Ma
The style of the Jōza no Ma is very typical of the mature *shoin* period and shows the standard prescription for a main *shoin*-style room except that it lacks a *chōdaigamae*. In the west wall are installed a *tokonoma* of a bay and a half, typically toward the veranda (south) side, and a one-bay shelf alcove to the north (pl. 111). The decorative lacquered molding of both are elevated above *tatami* level, and the lintel of the *tokonoma* is quite thick. The shelves are arranged in the tripartite *seirō-dana* style and include upper cabinets. The *tsukeshoin* transom has a delicate lattice with diamond-pattern 139

(*hanazama*) openwork carving, and the transom between the Jōza no Ma and the Ryūko no Ma anteroom includes carving in a multifoil shape inset into a grill transom background. This simple decor is standard for the period and makes the Guest Hall a very representative structure of the Kan'ei era (1624–44).

The Imperial Apartments and Denjō of the Former Ichijō-in

The Imperial Apartments and Denjō of the former Ichijō-in are good examples of Edo-period structures that retain elements of the *shinden* style. The Ichijō-in was originally built in the tenth century as a subsidiary temple of Kōfuku-ji in Nara, Japan's capital from 710 to 794. The Ichijō-in was a *monzeki* temple and thus of considerable importance. It suffered several conflagrations through its long history, the Imperial Apartments (Shinden), Denjō, and Genkan previous to the present ones having been destroyed by fire in 1642. The rebuilding of these structures was completed in 1650.

After the Meiji Restoration in 1868 the temple was deconsecrated. Thereafter known as the former Ichijō-in, the complex was variously used as a prefectural government office and, more recently, as a prefectural court building. In 1964, however, it was moved to the grounds of Tōshōdai-ji, another important temple of the Nara period, and rebuilt in its 1650 configuration on the basis of old plans. Now known as the Portrait Hall, it houses a dry lacquer statue of the blind Chinese prelate Chien Chen

111. *Tokonoma*, staggered shelves, and *tsukeshoin* of the Jōza no Ma; Guest Hall, Shōjū Raigō-ji.

THE EDO PERIOD

(Ganjin in Japanese; 688–763), the oldest extant portrait in sculpture of an actual figure in Japanese history.

Characteristics of the Plan

The main facade of the Imperial Apartments faces south, and two rows of rooms are located north and south behind it (pl. 112). The front row includes a large Imperial Hall (forty-nine mats), which occupies the eastern two-thirds of the south row, and the main room of the structure, the Jōdan no Ma (fourteen mats), which is located in the southwest corner. As befits its character as the main room, the Jōdan no Ma includes a two-bay *tokonoma* at the south side of the main (west) wall, and a one-bay shelf alcove beside it at the north.

The rear row of rooms at the north include the Ume no Ma (eight mats) at the east, the Matsu no Ma (twenty mats) at the center, and the Sakura no Ma (ten mats) at the west. The building is surrounded both by broad verandas and by outer verandas one step lower. The south and west sides as well are graced with an ornamental railing, and the center of the south main facade veranda has a railed staircase with a projecting eave overhead, all of which are older *shinden*-style elements (pl. 113).

The Denjō building stands to the southeast of the Imperial Apartments and is connected to it by an *ochima*, a small corridor with a low floor often used in *shinden*-style buildings (pl. 112). The south side of the Denjō holds the Denjō no Ma (thirty mats). At the north are the two Kujo no Ma (eighteen mats and twelve mats west to east). A broad veranda projects from the south side of the Denjō no Ma, and a *genkan* stands at the east side of the twelve-mat Kujo no Ma. Outer verandas one step lower flank all but the north side of the building.

The exteriors of both structures are composed mainly of sliding wooden doors (*mairado*). At the south side of the Denjō no Ma are swinging wooden doors, which together with the broad veranda give the Denjō no Ma the appearance of an entry-waiting room. This type of plan, like the details mentioned above, is related to the *shinden* rather than to the *shoin* style of building.

The Interior of the Jōdan no Ma

The Jōdan no Ma is furnished as a *shoin*-style audience hall, being one step raised and including a *tokonoma* and staggered shelves (pl. 114). It has, however, no *tsukeshoin* or *chōdaigamae*. The shelves exhibit the three-step *kasumi-dana* or "mist" design and are a simpler version of the *kasumi-dana* shelves of the Shugaku-in Detached Palace completed nine years after the Ichijō-in (pl. 157). The shelf alcove also includes a high floorboard, and upper cabinets as well. The room has, in sum, an up-to-date appearance for the age in which it was created.

The Jōdan no Ma is the only room in the complex with a coved and coffered

141

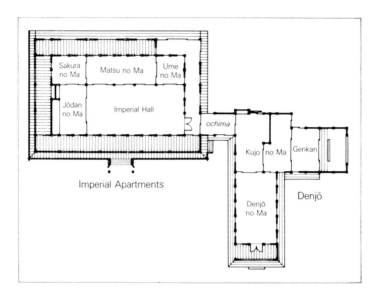

112. Plan of the Imperial Apartments and the Denjō of the former
Ichijō-in.

ceiling, though a simple coffered ceiling can be seen in the Sakura no Ma, a waiting room which is built on the level of the Jōdan no Ma. The mural paintings of the interior have all been lost, the only decorative touches remaining being the metal fittings of the shelves and the transom which has a diamond lattice with openwork carving.

In both exterior appearance and layout, the Imperial Apartments and Denjō bear a strong debt to the *shinden* style, a remarkable fact considering the date of construction of the building. This use of *shinden* elements can be partially explained, however, by the fact that the Ichijō-in was a *monzeki* temple, that is, one of those temples headed by a member of the imperial house or one of a select number of noble families. The *shinden* style, which developed during the court-centered Heian period, was regularly retained in imperial buildings even after the *shoin* style developed, and still today the Kyoto Imperial Palace in general reflects the *shinden* design. For example, a *denjō no ma* is also found on the southern veranda of the Seiryō-den residence in the Imperial Palace. The connection of the Ichijō-in *monzeki* with the court aristocracy thus perhaps accounts for the *shinden*-style elements retained in the structure, as it may, in fact, for the same phenomenon seen in the Sambō-in discussed in Chapter Three. *Shoin*-style *monzeki* temples do, however, exist as well, the Manshu-in being one such example.

113. The Imperial Apartments viewed from the southwest; former Ichijō-in.

114. *Tokonoma*, staggered shelves, and *chōdaigamae* of the Jōdan no Ma; Imperial Apartments, former Ichijō-in.

The Kaitoku-kan of Kōchi Castle

The construction of Kōchi Castle was begun in 1601 when Yamanouchi Kazutoyo (1546–1605), an ally of Tokugawa Ieyasu, took control of Tosa province (modern Kōchi Prefecture) after the battle of Sekigahara. The castle was completed in 1611. In 1727 it was destroyed by fire, but reconstruction was begun two years later, and was completed in 1753. The Kaitoku-kan was also lost in the 1727 conflagration, but was rebuilt between 1747 and 1749, according to a record discovered during repairs in 1959. It is felt, however, that the 1747 version was rebuilt along the lines of the 1611 structure. There is no other castle in Japan that still retains both its donjon and its palace.

The Plan

The Kaitoku-kan palace area, located to the southwest of the donjon, is composed of a Shikidai no Ma entry section and a Seiden (Main Hall; pl. 115). Access is gained by first entering the Hommaru Compound, then proceeding to the *genkan* entrance area west of the donjon. Entering the Shikidai no Ma (pl. 116), one then proceeds south through a nine-mat room to the Yon no Ma (twelve mats), the northwest of the four major spaces in the Main Hall proper. These spaces form a rough rectangle, with two rows of two rooms each, the southern row constituting the main facade. This southern row is composed of the San no Ma (twelve mats) to the west and the Ni no Ma (eight mats) to the east. North of the Ni no Ma is the major room of the Main Hall, the Jōdan no Ma (eight mats). The minor spaces of the Main Hall include a four-mat fixed-wall storage space (*nando*) located between the Jōdan no Ma and the

144

115. *Genkan* entrance to the Shikidai; Kai-toku-kan, Kōchi Castle (donjon in background).

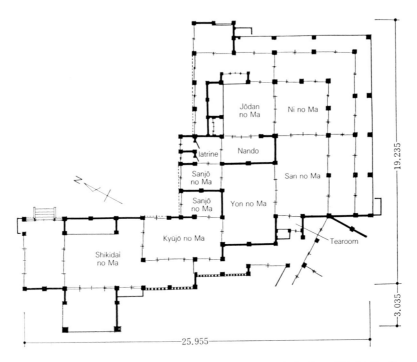

116. Plan of the Kaitoku-kan, Kōchi Castle.

Yon no Ma, two rooms to the north of the Yon no Ma of three mats each, and a tea-room west of the San no Ma. North of the storage area is a latrine, and on the eastern veranda is an entrance to the donjon. This plan, though drawn in 1747, reflects that of the original Keichō-era (1596–1615) castle, and thus provides an early example of the type of *shoin* that developed in a castle compound.

Elements of the Jōdan no Ma

The main wall of the main room, the Jōdan no Ma, incorporates a *tokonoma* and staggered shelves arranged in the standard manner with the *tokonoma* the closer to the *tatami* corridor and veranda (pl. 117). While the decorative molding of the *tokonoma* is of late style, resting as it does directly on the *tatami* mats, the staggered shelves are of an old style, having only two levels. On the west wall of the room is a *chōdaigamae* which lets into the storage space. It is built after the old style, with two doors fixed in place flanking the two sliding central doors. The requisite *tsukeshoin* across from the *chōdaigamae* is also in evidence, and it includes a late-style ogee-arched window (pl. 118). The *shōji* also show a late design in their use of low wainscoting.

While various details of the room thus show post-1615 designs, the basic appearance of the main room recalls early styles. While it can be surmised that the Jōdan no Ma was also used for audiences, the presence of a tearoom and latrine gives the building the character of a daimyo living quarters. In sum, besides being the only remaining castle to have both a donjon and a palace extant, Kōchi Castle is, like the Ichijō-in, an important example of a building consciously recreating the style of an earlier era.　145

117. Jōdan no Ma of the Kaitoku-kan, Kōchi Castle.

118. *Tokonoma* and *tsukeshoin* of the Jōdan no Ma; Kaitoku-kan, Kōchi Castle.

5

THE SUKIYA SHOIN

The *sukiya* was originally a room or house in which to drink tea. As the tea ceremony became an established part of upper-class life, elements of the rustic teahouse came to be incorporated into the *shoin* scheme, resulting in the mellow and approachable *sukiya shoin* or *sukiya* style.

The simple process of preparing and drinking tea developed over the ages in Japan into a ritual of great beauty and sophistication. The motions for mixing the green powder and hot water, presenting the tea bowl to the guest, drinking the tea, and appreciating the utensils and room decor differ according to school and level of formality but are in every case minutely prescribed. Out of the discipline and concentration required for the performance by host and guest springs a spiritual tranquility and a feeling of respect for and harmony with all in the room and with all things. The utensils used in the ceremony, the building in which it takes place, and the surrounding garden all enter into the ceremony and contribute to its ideals of purity, restraint, and naturalness. The aesthetic refinement of the *cha no yu* has thus deeply influenced not only architecture but all of Japanese art.

Powdered tea was introduced into Japan in the Kamakura period (1185–1332) as a stimulant for Zen monks. Tea drinking later became an upper-class entertainment, with elegant and ostentatious gatherings often held at Ashikaga Yoshimitsu's Kitayama Villa for tasting various teas and gaming at guessing the origins thereof. Yoshimitsu's descendant Yoshimasa enjoyed "palace tea," wherein the beverage was prepared in a separate area and then transported to a formal-style guest room for consumption. This formal reception room usually included the *shoin*-style *tokonoma*, staggered shelves, and *tsukeshoin*, which were adorned with precious objects of art.

It was during the time of Yoshimasa that Murata Jukō (1422–1502), "the father of the tea ceremony," combined the austerity and spiritual discipline of Zen tea with the artistic and cultural refinement of Yoshimasa and his circle. In Jukō's ceremony, tea was made and consumed in the same room, a small space of four and a half mats. Takeno Jōō (1502–55) and Sen no Rikyū (1522–91) developed the tea ceremony and teahouses to their most simple and rustic form. It was under these tea masters that roughly finished walls and bamboo lattice ceilings, coarse posts, and garden walks came to be used. Rikyū's "grass huts" (*sōan*) eliminated all ostentation and super-

147

fluity, being small in area and employing natural woods, thatched roofs, and wattled windows to create an atmosphere of profound simplicity, of *wabi* which is "poverty surpassing riches." But inherent to this simplicity was painstaking consideration behind each dimension and behind the placement of each post and each window. At the core of the simplest tearooms was the *daimegamae*—the server's three-quarter-length *daime* mat and the center post (*nakabashira*), which stands at one corner of the sunken hearth (*ro*).

Rikyū also mixed *sōan* elements with those of the formal *shoin* style in his larger *hiroma* tearooms. It was from this amalgamation that the *sukiya shoin* was created.

After Rikyū, two members of the daimyo class, Furuta Oribe (1544–1615) and Kobori Enshū (1579–1647), continued the relaxation of boundaries between the *shoin* and the *sōan*. By the second quarter of the seventeenth century the combination of the two styles was well advanced, and the resultant *sukiya shoin* had become the standard mode of building for private residential areas. But formal *shoin* structures and completely rustic *sōan* continued to be built as well.

It was in the seventeenth century as well that the formal and informal rooms in residences became once again consolidated under one roof rather than located in separate buildings as they had been at the Ninomaru Palace of Nijō Castle. Concurrently, elements of the *shoin* style began to permeate the lower levels of society, beginning with the houses of village headmen and also those of the wealthy merchants who, though at the bottom of the Confucian social hierarchy as defined by the government, were, nevertheless, attaining a position of financial dominance. These *minka* homes will be discussed in the following chapter.

The Ryūkō-in Shoin

The Ryūkō-in (alternately Ryōkō-in) is one of the many subtemples of the Daitoku-ji Zen temple in Kyoto. It is famous primarily for its tearoom, the Mittan no Seki, said to have been designed with the help of the great builder and tea master Kobori Enshū. It was begun in 1606 by Kuroda Nagamasa (1568–1623) for the repose of his father, Yoshitaka (1546–1604), whose grave is on the site, and was designated the Ryūkō-in after Yoshitaka's posthumous name. Nagamasa served with Hideyoshi in Kyushu and in Korea, and fought at Sekigahara with Ieyasu, by whom he was afterwards rewarded with the immense Chikuzen fief in northern Kyushu.

The original Ryūkō-in complex included an abbot's quarters, which was dismantled in the early Meiji period (1868–1912). The present Shoin also appears to have been known by comparison as the Kohōjō (Secondary Abbot's Quarters) and was reserved for private use. Both structures were most likely completed by 1608. The teahouse, the Mittan no Seki, however, is thought to date from 1628 to 1640, and there is evidence as well that it was not built originally as part of the Shoin but was instead free-standing.

The Ryūkō-in Shoin has a two-row plan (pl. 119). That of the south contains the Ichi no Ma (ten mats) to the west and the Ni no Ma (eight mats) to the east. The northern row includes the Rokujō no Ma (six mats) to the east and the Mittan no Seki to the west. Verandas or corridors skirt all but the east side of the building, and an area for washing and storing tea utensils (*mizuya*) is located at the northeast.

Although the Ichi no Ma is the main room of the structure, it includes only a *tokonoma*, this on the side opposite the veranda (pl. 120). Both the eccentric placement of this *tokonoma* and the absence of the staggered shelves and *tsukeshoin* normally included in a standard *shoin* room show the Ryūkō-in Shoin to have been built in the *sukiya* vein.

The Mittan no Seki

The Mittan no Seki, along with the Bōsen of the Kohō-an to be discussed in the following section, typify the tearoom style of Kobori Enshū, one of the central figures of the Kan'ei era (1624–44). He was Titular Governor of Tōtōmi province (part of present-day Shizuoka Prefecture), then lord of Matsuyama in Iyo province (present-day Ehime Prefecture), and was in the service of the first three Tokugawa shoguns. Active in a vast range of artistic activities, he was the quintessential *sukisha* or man of taste. As Commissioner of Construction for the Tokugawa and Magistrate for much of the Kyoto-Osaka area, he made major contributions to the building of the Imperial Palace, the Sentō Palace for Retired Emperor Gomizunoo and his consort, and the castles of Nagoya, Fushimi, Nijō, Edo, and Mito. He was skilled as well in painting, flower arrangement, poetry, and ceramics. Furthermore, he taught tea to the shogun Iemitsu and developed not only the Enshū style of "daimyo tea," but his own style of teahouse architecture to accompany it.

Not as severe as Rikyū's tea ceremony, Enshū's canon allowed for refined and costly tea ceremony objects given names redolent of classical learning. Nor were Enshū's tea gatherings confined to one room as they had been with Rikyū. Rather he, like Oribe, might schedule the drinking of the heavy formal tea in the teahouse, then move to the *kusari no ma*, between the *shoin* and the teahouse, and offer light informal tea and relaxed conversation. There was often a banquet in the *shoin* as well, and these rooms would be characterized by a fusion of rustic teahouse elements with those of the formal and spacious *shoin* style. The combination of Enshū's increased emphasis on the entertainment aspects of tea and his use of the *shoin* style with rich and varied ornamentation is said to reflect *kirei sabi* (refined rusticity), and as such had great appeal for the upper echelons of the military class.

The Mittan no Seki derives its name from a calligraphic scroll, painted by the Southern Sung Ch'an (Zen) monk Mi-an Hsien-chieh (Japanese: Mittan Kanketsu), which is hung in the room's *tokonoma*. The chamber is four and a half mats, plus a *daime*, a *daime* mat being three-quarters the length of a regular mat and often used in teahouse and *sukiya shoin* architecture. From the point of view of the tea ceremony, 149

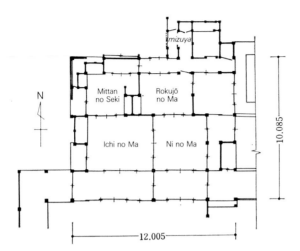

119. Plan of the Ryūkō-in Shoin, Daitoku-ji.

the core of the room is the *daimegamae*, consisting of the *daime* mat for the tea server at the east, and the sunken hearth with center post set at the hearth's southeast corner (pl. 121). The *daimegamae* is prominently situated and lit by a line of wainscoted *shōji*.

A partial wall (*sodekabe*) connects the center post to the *tokonoma*, called the Mittan-doko, at the south (pl. 121). Diagonally across at the northwest is the *tatami*-floored main *tokonoma*, in which is hung a letter written by Rikyū (pl. 122). The two *tokonoma* lend the room an unusual flavor and have led to the supposition that the Mittan-doko, with its high wooden floorboard, was built originally as a *tsukeshoin*. This seems quite likely as it is recorded that in 1641 the Mittan calligraphy was not hung in the Mittan-doko but instead in the main *tokonoma*.

Adjacent to the main *tokonoma* is a shelf alcove of unique and fanciful design (pls. 122, 123). The floorboard is elevated, and tall cabinets support a strut into which tie the shelves, two lower shelves to the right and one higher to the left, in an arrangement of balanced asymmetry. The openwork carving marks them as being to Enshū's taste. Both the lower and upper cabinets have paintings by Shōkadō Shōjō. That he was not active as a painter until after 1615 supports the dating of the Mittan no Seki to the Kan'ei era (1624–44).

The posts on the east and south sides of the room are planed square in the standard *shoin* manner. The *shoin* style is seen as well in the inclusion of the mid-wall frieze rails and wainscoted *shōji*. The light and original design of these *shōji*, however, make them appropriate for a *sukiya* structure. The posts of the north and west walls are in the *sukiya* style, being of the *menkawa* type with unplaned corners. The Mittan no Seki thus incorporates both strict *shoin* and naturalistic teahouse elements, making it a fine example of the *sukiya shoin* style.

150

120. *Tokonoma* of the Ichi no Ma; Ryūkō-in Shoin, Daitoku-ji.

121. Mittan-doko of the Mittan no Seki; Ryūkō-in Shoin, Daitoku-ji. 151

122. *Tokonoma* and staggered
shelves of the Mittan no Seki;
Ryūkō-in Shoin, Daitoku-ji.

123. Staggered shelves of the Mittan no Seki; Ryūkō-in Shoin, Daitoku-ji.

THE KOHŌ-AN

The Kohō-an, with its Bōsen tearoom, and the Ryūkō-in Shoin with its Mittan no Seki, are the best extant examples of Kobori Enshū's teahouse style. A subtemple of Daitoku-ji, the Kohō-an was built as Enshū's family temple and was originally located along with the Mittan no Seki on the grounds of the Ryūkō-in. Constructed in 1612 it was, like the Mittan no Seki, built during the tenure of the abbot Kōgetsu. In 1641, or the year after, the structure was moved to a more distant location, and the Hōjō, Shoin, and Bōsen tearoom are believed to have been completed by 1643. Enshū, however, who took as a personal epithet the name Kohōan, was able to enjoy his creation for only four years before his death in 1647.

One hundred and fifty years later, in 1793, all the major buildings on the site save the front gate were lost in a conflagration. The abbot of Daitoku-ji at that time, Kankai, requested the Konoe family and the lord of Matsue, Matsudaira Harusato (1751–1818), to aid in the rebuilding. The choice of Harusato, better known by his Zen name, Fumai, was a good one, as his introduction to tea had been in the Enshū style.

Fumai was, in fact, one of the foremost tea practitioners of his age, a scholar who thoroughly investigated all the major schools of tea and contributed original ideas on the subject as well. Tea historian and connoisseur, his collection of renowned wares, the Unshū Meibutsu, was larger than any collection accumulated previously. On his death in 1818, he was buried at the Kohō-an. It was in that year as well that, according to an extant ridgepole certificate, rebuilding of the major structures was completed.

The Shoin

The plan of the main Shoin is square, and is composed of four rooms, with two auxiliary rooms to the east (pl. 124). The main room, the Jikinyū-ken (eight mats) is at the southwest, and the Tsugi no Ma anteroom (six mats) borders it to the east. Both these rooms open on to a veranda at the south. North of the Jikinyū-ken is the San'un-shō tearoom (five and a half mats), with a Butsuma (four and a half mats) to the east.

The plan of the major space is thus quite close to that of the Ryūkō-in Shoin (pl. 119). The San'un-shō tearoom, in fact, is said to have been patterned on the Mittan no Seki, and although minor variations are in evidence, the overall appearance of the room reflects the Enshū style. A *daime tokonoma* is located on the north wall, and the *daimegamae*, with sunken hearth, center post, and *tsuridana* ("hung shelves"), is diagonally across at the southeast. Details of the design may have been slightly altered, however, during the rebuilding.

The combination of Jikinyū-ken (main room) and Tsugi no Ma (anteroom) is designed in the *sukiya shoin* style. The inclusion of a *tokonoma*, *tsukeshoin*, and staggered shelves herein is appropriate to a *shoin* building, and the location thereof, with the *tokonoma* and *tsukeshoin* on the far wall of the main room (pl. 125) and the staggered shelves directly across from these on the east wall of the anteroom, shows the imaginative informal taste inherent to the *sukiya*. The *sukiya* style is also seen in the frieze rails, the edges of which show a slight bevel.

As at the Ryūkō-in Shoin, the *tokonoma* is positioned on the far side of the wall from the veranda. The *tsukeshoin* is thus located in the old fashion, closer to the outside, providing illumination for the desk area. Old styles are seen as well in the use of a grill transom between the Jikinyū-ken and the Tsugi no Ma and in the shelf alcove which has a quite narrow width (one-half bay) and shelves which are set relatively high. The retention of the old style is probably to recreate the personal taste of Enshū.

The Bōsen Tearoom

One of the finest extant examples of a tearoom of *shoin* lineage, the Bōsen was rebuilt after the 1793 fire in a manner very close to the original. Located between the Hōjō and the Shoin, the room is twelve mats in area, these irregular in placement (pl. 126). The frieze rails and square posts contribute to its overall *shoin* feeling. This effect is softened, however, by the inclusion of informal tea-style elements such as the *menkawa*

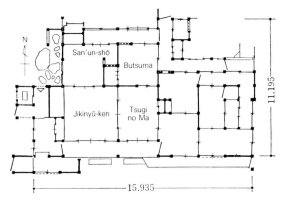

124. Plan of the Kohō-an, Daitoku-ji.

125. *Tokonoma* and *tsukeshoin* of the Jikinyū-ken; Kohō-an, Daitoku-ji.   155

126. Bōsen tearoom, Kohō-an, Daitoku-ji.

post with unplaned corners, the low *shōji* window to the left of the *tokonoma*, and in the simplification of the *tokonoma* itself through the use of the frieze rail as the *tokonoma* lintel rather than adding the usual *tokonoma* lintel at a different height. The slight bevel of the frieze rail edges and the sand-rubbed (*sunazuri*) ceiling as well help create a mellow appearance.

It is in the west side of the room, however, that the true tea nature of the space is best felt. The transom and upper wall are composed of *shōji*, and the lower half, below the middle runner, is left open to the outside (pl. 127). This ingenious design both protects the room from the glare of the western sun and presents the garden beyond as if through a picture frame. It shows a consummate understanding of both these elements and results in an intimate union of the tearoom with the surrounding natural environment. Although this tearoom can be entered directly from the Shoin and the Abbot's Quarters, it is possible to enter via the garden as in the thatched cottage (*sōan*) tea structures of Jōō and Rikyū. Guests to the Bōsen tea ceremony can follow the same route they would at a *sōan* tea gathering, proceeding over the flat stones of the garden walk to the stone on which footwear is removed, passing the stone lantern and low

156

127. The Jikinyū-ken garden from the open west wall of the Bōsen tearoom; Kohō-an, Dai-toku-ji.

handwashing basin on the way. From here the guests enter the room itself via the low outside veranda and then the wider and higher veranda. Entered in this way, the open lower half of the wall serves the same function as the low entrance (*nijiriguchi*) to a *sōan*-style tearoom, causing the guest to bow down on entering, thus contributing to the attitude of humility required for the tea ceremony. This open-walled design is often referred to as the "boat-mooring" style.

The design of the Bōsen tearoom thus blends the *shoin* style with that of the *sōan* thatched teahouse, creating at once a style appropriate to the simple and naturalistic atmosphere of tea as well as to the taste of the daimyo. Enshū's conception, which combines a tea participant's emphasis on spiritual calm with his own classical erudition, is symbolized by the name of the room itself. Literally meaning "Forget the Net," the term "Bōsen" is taken from the proverb of the Chinese Taoist sage Chuang Tzu which reads "Catch the fish, then forget the net," a metaphor suggesting the way to achieve complete inner serenity through grasping the inner meaning of things and forgetting the formal outer aspects. Clearly the goal of the proverb and design of the Bōsen tearoom and garden beyond are perfectly compatible.

157

THE SHOIN OF THE MANSHU-IN

Like many Japanese buildings of long and distinguished history, the Manshu-in (alternately, Manju-in) has been relocated several times since it was first constructed. The temple is generally believed to have originally been located on Mount Hiei, and then to have been moved twice more, the second time to Kyoto proper. In 1656 it was moved for the last time to its present site, near the famous Shugaku-in Detached Palace. Since the middle ages the Manshu-in has been designated a *monzeki* temple of the Tendai sect. Because it is located in Ichijō-ji Takenouchi-chō, the temple is consequently often known as the Takenouchi Monzeki. The chief priest's position at the time of the final move was filled by Ryōshō (1622–93), second son of Prince Hachijō-no-miya Toshihito (1579–1629), who began the building of Katsura Detached Palace. Ryōshō was, like his father, a man of deep artistic appreciation, having copied *The Tale of Genji* and other classics, as well as having studied painting under Kanō Tan'yū (1602–74), creator of much of the *fusuma* art in the Ninomaru Palace and one of the most eminent members of the Kanō school, official painters to the shogunate.

Besides the Shoin (pl. 128), the present Manshu-in complex includes a Hondō and temple kitchens, and the Hassō-ken (or Hassō-seki) teahouse. Because the date 1656 was discovered on a *fusuma* frame, it is thought that all four buildings date from that time. Both the Shoin and the Hondō are Important Cultural Properties. The present appearance of the temple is, however, somewhat different from that of the seventeenth century, for in 1872 the Imperial Apartments on the grounds were dismantled and a *butsuma* (devotional chamber) was added to the Hondō. Before this time the Hondō was known as the Ōjoin or Major Shoin, and traces of a four-mat *jōdan* and a *tsukeshoin* that were removed when the Butsuma was added are still to be found. The Hondō retains, however, the general Ōjoin plan. It was in 1872 as well that the Koshoin (Minor Shoin) was renamed the Shoin, the name by which it is known today.

Characteristics of the Interior

The Shoin was used as the living area of the Manshu-in, and its rooms are consequently of a more private character than those of the Hondō, the public area of the complex. The main room of the Shoin is the Tasogare no Ma (seven mats), located in the center of the building's east side (pl. 129). The Fuji no Ma (anteroom; eight mats) borders it to the southeast. To the west, five-mat (Gojō no Ma) and two-mat (Nijō no Ma) rooms for preparing tea, as well as a three-mat room, are arranged north to south. Behind the Tasogare no Ma is the Hassō-ken teahouse, three mats plus a *daime* in size, and a *mizuya nagashi* for washing and storing tea utensils. In general this arrangement is well suited to a living area.

The Tasogare no Ma is constructed in a softened and mellowed version of the *shoin* style. A *jōdan* of two *daime*-sized mats is located in the northeast corner with a *tokonoma* and *tsukeshoin* located therein (pl. 132). West of this *jōdan* area is a shelf alcove (pl. 133). These elements all show imaginative and painstaking workmanship, as does the tran-

158

128. South facade of the Shoin, Manshu-in.

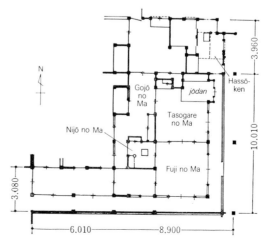

129. Plan of the Shoin, Manshu-in.

159

130. Tasogare no Ma viewed from the Fuji no Ma;
Manshu-in Shoin.

som between the Tasogare no Ma and the Fuji no Ma (pl. 130). It is a complex design, with two rows of carved chrysanthemums in a variety of colors, alternately carved in openwork and bas-relief. The flowers are interspersed in a zigzag pattern within a gridlike latticework. Even the design of the veranda railing shows considerable forethought and care (pl. 128). When compared to the *tokonoma*, staggered shelves, and transom of the Hondō (the old Major Shoin) the lightness of the details of the Shoin is immediately apparent.

The Manshu-in also includes facilities for two very different styles of tea ceremonies. The Hassō-ken, located to the north of the *jōdan* area, is entered via a low door from the garden to the east (pl. 129). It is designed in a style having much in common with that of Enshū, already described in the discussions of the Mittan no Seki of the Ryūkō-in and Bōsen of the Kohō-an.

Far more noteworthy are the facilities for preparing tea in the two-mat tearoom (Nijō no Ma) west of the Fuji no Ma (pl. 131). At the center of the floor is a sunken hearth and diagonally across from it at the northwest is a floor-level cupboard for

131. The two-mat tearoom (Nijō no Ma) of the Shoin, Manshu-in.

storing tea utensils. Across from this at the southwest is a small *tokonoma* with an abbreviated post topped with an inverted, carved lotus bulb. This post is connected to the wall post by a plank (*sodeita*) with carved openwork designs. The walls are papered and the two panels on the floor-level cupboard are decorated with ink paintings. Traces of paintings remain on the walls as well. The low ceiling is constructed with *shoin*-style battens (*saobuchi*). The decor is thus of *shoin* type, far removed from the *sōan* style of Rikyū.

The special relationship of this two-mat room to the rooms beside it recalls the early "palace tea" ceremony, wherein tea was prepared by a retainer in a separate room and then brought to the master in the main room for consumption. Although there are no records confirming how the Manshu-in two-mat room functioned, it is quite likely that it was used in the palace tea style. It combines with the refined and painstakingly crafted *sukiya shoin* cast of the Tasogare no Ma and Fuji no Ma to provide a very representative example of the residential architecture favored by the court aristocracy of the early Edo period.

161

132. *Jōdan* of the Tasogare no Ma, Manshu-in Shoin.
Two *daime* mats in size, the *jōdan* of the Tasogare no Ma is bordered by a lacquered molding (*kamachi*). Its ceiling has been lowered as well, further accentuating this area. The *tsukeshoin* includes an ogee-arched window and, beneath the writing surface, a small recessed wall (*kegomi-ita*) with an elegantly decorated border. The addition of a *tsukeshoin* gives to this *jōdan* a study-area quality.

133. Tasogare no Ma, Manshu-in Shoin.
The main room of the Manshu-in Shoin, the Tasogare no Ma, has a private, living-area quality. On the main wall are a *jōdan* area and shelves, the latter having a very original design. The incorporation of a small cupboard in the center of the assemblage is a particularly novel touch. The room is clearly in the *sukiya shoin* style, the posts having unplaned corners, and the ceiling battens being quite thin.

163

THE SUKIYA SHOIN STYLE AT NISHI HONGAN-JI

The Hiunkaku

The Hiunkaku is famous along with the Kinkaku and the Ginkaku as a particularly fine example of multistoried pavilion architecture (pl. 134). But whereas the latter two were built in the Muromachi period (1333–1567) and show only isolated elements of the *shoin* style, the Hiunkaku has a mature *shoin* design, with elements of the *sukiya shoin* style in evidence as well.

The three-story structure is in the center of the Tekisui Garden at the southeast of the temple compound and faces north over the Hōrō Pond. The same type of building as the Kinkaku but more complex, the Hiunkaku is said to have been moved from Hideyoshi's Juraku-dai castle-palace (1586–87), but it seems more likely that it was newly built in the Genna era (1615–24).

Included in the first floor are the Shōken-den main room (twenty-eight mats; pl. 135) and the Hakkei no Ma (twenty-four mats; pl. 139) which functions as an anteroom (pl. 140). The Funairi no Ma is included as well, with steps running below the floor level into the pond. The Ikujaku tearoom, added in later years, and a number of subsidiary spaces to the south, completes the plan of the first floor.

The Shōken-den served as a living quarters for the head priest, and could also be used for informal interviews. Light and airy in appearance, the room exhibits a richly innovative *shoin* configuration, one of the touchstones of *sukiya* influence. The seven and a half mats in the northwest are raised as a *jōdan*, the main wall incorporating a *tokonoma* of two and a half bays (pl. 141). North of this *jōdan* is a three-mat *jōjōdan* that projects into the *tatami*-covered corridor running between the veranda and the main rooms (pl. 136). On the northern wall of the *jōjōdan* is a *tsukeshoin* of one and a half bays. The proportions of the posts and frieze rails of the Shōken-den are comparatively thin, and this, plus the very imaginative and fanciful placement and form of the design elements, reflects the influence of the *sukiya* style.

The second floor room is known as the Kasen no Ma by virtue of the thirty-six *kasen* ("poetic geniuses") painted on the wooden doors. It is divided into a *jōdan* of eight mats and a lower level of eighteen, including the stairs. There are, however, none of the standard *shoin* accoutrements in this *jōdan*, which may imply it was used as a sleeping area. Above this floor is the Tekisei-rō, the "Turret to Pluck the Stars." Of its eight mats, one holds a *tokonoma* of later period. The two windows to the north and the two to the east show the military-fan-shaped (*gumbaigata*) ogee-arched design and give the room a watchtower aspect.

In sum, the Hiunkaku well exemplifies the light and airy quality of multistoried pavilion architecture. Its style can as well be classified as garden architecture, with various qualities of a detached country mansion incorporated as well. Its rich stylistic variation shows too the early stages of *sukiya*-style influence.

164

135 (following page, top). Shōken-den of the Hiunkaku, Nishi Hongan-ji.
The *jōdan* of the Shōken-den has a *tokonoma* of very original style. It is fitted with three *shōji* screens, the middle section having a lowered lintel with a wainscoted window beneath. This type of *jōdan*, built for the personal use of the head priest, has a very different atmosphere than the *shoin* structures of the military class.

136 (following page, bottom). *Jōjōdan* of the Shōken-den; Hiunkaku, Nishi Hongan-ji.
Located at the north side of the Shōken-den *jōdan*, the *jōjōdan* overlooks the Hōrō Pond. The window of the *tsukeshoin*, shown here with its *shōji* screens closed, is particularly striking, being done in the multifoiled (*kōzama*) style, its side frames of decoratively curved design. It adds an element of originality to both the interior and exterior. The west wall includes an ogee-arched window. Although no shelves are included, the *jōjōdan* definitely has a study-area atmosphere.

135–36. See preceding page for captions.

137–38. See following page for captions.

137 (preceding page, top). *Tokonoma* and *tsuke-shoin* of the Ichi no Ma; Kuroshoin, Nishi Hongan-ji.

Although the main wall of a *shoin* usually incorporates a *tokonoma* and staggered shelves, a *tsukeshoin* has been used instead of shelves on the main wall of the Kuroshoin. This arrangement, also seen in the Kohō-an Jikinyū-ken is that of a private living area. The position of the *tsuke-shoin* behind the *tokonoma* enables it to be used as a study area.

138 (preceding page, bottom). Ichi no Ma of the Kuroshoin, Nishi Hongan-ji.

One of the finest *sukiya shoin* in existence, the Kuroshoin of Nishi Hongan-ji was used as a living area and for private interviews. The intricacy of the impeccably crafted shelves, the ogee-arched window, and the rough corners of the posts show the more formal nature of these rooms in comparison to the Shiroshoin. The frieze rails, chamfered rather than cut at right angles, emphasize the relaxed character of the structure as well.

168   139. Hakkei no Ma viewed from the Shōken-den; Hiunkaku, Nishi Hongan-ji.

140. Plan of the first floor of the Hiunkaku, Nishi Hongan-ji.

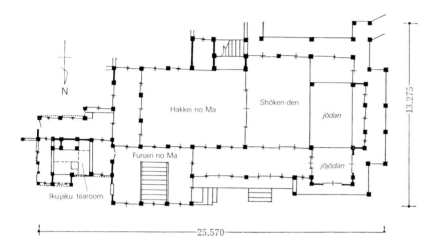

141. *Jōdan* and *jōjōdan* of the Shōken-den; Hiunkaku, Nishi Hongan-ji.   169

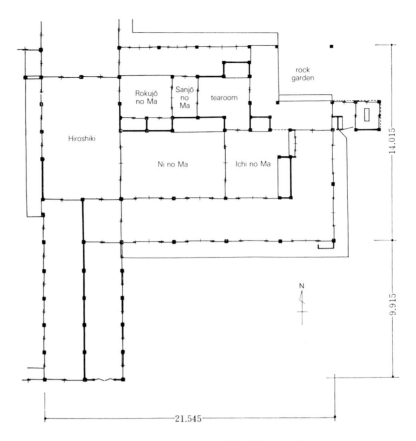

Sanjō
no
Ma

Rokujō
no Ma

tearoom

rock
garden

Hiroshiki

Ni no Ma

Ichi no Ma

14.015

N

9.915

21.545

142. Plan of the Kuroshoin, Nishi Hongan-ji.

The Kuroshoin

A more developed, nearly mature phase of the *sukiya shoin* is seen in the Nishi Hon-gan-ji Kuroshoin, designated a National Treasure. The structure is important not only aesthetically but historically as well, as its date of construction, 1656–57, is verified in temple records. Located to the northeast of the Shoin complex (pl. 96), it is connected to the Shiroshoin veranda by a double-row corridor. The Kuroshoin has, like the Shiroshoin (pl. 97), a two-row plan (pl. 142), but here it is the south row that contains the main rooms—the Ichi no Ma (eleven mats) to the east and the Ni no Ma (twenty mats) to the west. The northern row includes a tearoom (seven mats) at the east, then to the west the Sanjō no Ma (three mats), Rokujō no Ma (Kusari no Ma; six mats), and the Hiroshiki (twenty-seven mats). A *tatami*-covered veranda borders the south side of the building, and a roofed garden space occupies the northeast corner.

But though the two-row nature of the plan resembles that of the Shiroshoin, the character of the building is very different. At the east side of the Ichi no Ma is a one-and-a-half-bay *tokonoma* flanked by a *tsukeshoin* of one bay (pl. 137). A shelf alcove (one bay) is located at the north (pls. 138, 143), with a one-bay *renjimado*, a window

143. Staggered shelves of the Ichi no Ma;
Kuroshoin, Nishi Hongan-ji.

inset with regularly spaced vertical and horizontal slats, flanking it to the east. Outside the window is a small rock garden completely protected by overhanging eaves
(far left in plate 144). There are *tokonoma* at the north side of the Ni no Ma and on
the same side of the tearoom as well (pl. 145–46).

The details of these elements, though, make the most definite departure from the
polychromed magnificence of the Shiroshoin. The shelves of the Ichi no Ma are of
three-tiered design, suspended by struts from the cabinets above them (pl. 143).
They resemble the shelves of the Imperial Apartments of the Daigo-ji Sambō-in (pl.
48) in that they are free of the back wall of the alcove and have openwork carvings
in the wood backings. Their design is delicate and quite decorative. The fragile nature
of the shelves is reflected in the slender latticework of the transom between the Ichi
no Ma and the Ni no Ma (pl. 146), and in the *saobuchi* battens of the ceiling, which
are finished in the rough and natural *menkawa* style with unplaned corners. The posts
of the room are also finished in this fashion, except for the corner posts, which are
of the square type. The location of the *tsukeshoin* also reflects *sukiya* trends, being
innovatively recessed into the corner between the north slatted window and the east
tokonoma. These elements, in sum, lend the building a decidedly private, living-area
quality.

144. North facade of the Kuroshoin, Nishi Hongan-ji.

145. Tearoom of the Kuroshoin, Nishi Hongan-ji.

146. Ni no Ma of the Kuroshoin, Nishi Hongan-ji. 173

KATSURA DETACHED PALACE

The Katsura Detached Palace is the finest *sukiya shoin* remaining in Japan. Its main complex blends with a splendid pond and garden that includes priceless rocks, trees, and lanterns, as well as four teahouses, a small shrine, and various subsidiary structures. Built over nearly half a century, the main complex is composed of three major sections, the Old Shoin, Middle Shoin, and New Palace, these arranged in a zigzag plan receding from the west edge of the pond (pl. 147). Together they show a progression from early to mature *sukiya shoin* design, and provide an important example of a completely realized villa plan.

It was this palace in particular that inspired the German architect Bruno Taut to call on the Japanese of the 1930s to temper their efforts to adopt Western architecture with a renewed appreciation of their own cultural heritage. Today this structure more than any other is popularly held to be the quintessence of Japanese traditional domestic architecture.

Katsura was begun by Prince Hachijō-no-miya Toshihito (1579–1629) sometime in the second decade of the seventeenth century. The prince's life was intertwined with the politics of his day, the turbulent Momoyama and early Edo periods. He was adopted by Toyotomi Hideyoshi in 1586 as the heir to the theretofore childless general, but this relationship was dissolved three years later when Hideyoshi's mistress bore him a child of his own. By way of consolation, the prince was allowed to form a new branch of the imperial line, becoming in 1590 Prince Hachijō-no-miya and taking the personal name Toshihito. He was also granted land and a generous stipend. Katsura Village eventually became part of these lands granted to the prince. This was located near the west bank of the Katsura River in the southwest suburbs of Kyoto.

A number of written sources suggest that by 1616 Prince Toshihito had built some type of retreat at this location. Thereafter the prince gradually entered deeper into political life, serving as something of an intermediary between the court and the shogunate. The number of visitors to his retreat consequently increased and the buildings and gardens became well known as a place of cultural importance.

It was once thought that the entire garden was designed by the great Kobori Enshū and that Toshihito told him to use as much time and money on the project as was necessary and not to unveil it to him until it was completed. Although there is no proof that Toshihito ever offered these conditions, the design is clearly influenced by Enshū's style. Some scholars assert that the great artist was directly involved from the first, and others that he contributed to the later building campaign of Toshitada, Toshihito's son.

After the prince's death in 1629 the early Katsura palace was allowed to deteriorate. Lavish support from the shogunate after about 1640, however, made it possible for Toshitada (1619–62, also called Noritada) to rebuild the palace. It appears that

147. The Shoin complex, Katsura Detached Palace.

the present Old Shoin was part of Toshihito's villa and that the Middle Shoin was completed in about 1641–42 by his son. Other theories, however, hold that the Old Shoin and Middle Shoin complexes were built simultaneously during the first construction campaign, or that the Middle Shoin was built first and the Old Shoin moved to its present site later from some other location.

Thereafter it appears that Toshitada began concentrating on the garden and teahouses, examining tea structures in various parts of Japan for inspiration. By 1649 there were five teahouses in the garden, the Geppa-rō, Shōkin-tei, Shōka-tei, Shōi-ken, and the Chikurin-tei (the last no longer extant), as well as various subsidiary structures. Much of the garden was designed to call to mind famous places in classical literature. The Geppa-rō, located quite near the main *shoin* complex, is built on an artificial hill overlooking the pond. L-shaped in plan, the structure has no ceiling, as is the case with many teahouses, but the underside of the roof is more ornamental than usual, and has at once a rustic and a refined appearance. Across the pond from the Geppa-rō is the Shōkin-tei, known for its checkerboard blue and white painting on the *tokonoma* and *fusuma*. It is composed of a number of rooms, and appears to have been built in more than one stage. Close by are two pavilions, the Sotokoshikake and the Manji-tei, which serve as annexes for the Shōkin-tei. Next in order along the path

175

around the pond is the Shōka-tei, built on the highest ground of the villa. A small structure resembling a mountain rest house, it appears to have been transferred from the main residence of the Hachijō-no-miya family. Further on is the Onrin-dō, a small shrine dedicated to the Hachijō-no-miya ancestors. The path leads finally to the Shōi-ken, another large teahouse that may have been used as an independent dwelling. It is famous especially for its wall design in velvet, an exotic material at the time. These teahouses are all splendid structures and, were there space, a chapter could be profitably devoted to them alone.

The circumstances under which the New Palace was built are unclear, some scholars asserting that it was built for Toshitada's adopted son, Prince Yasuhito, and others holding, in light of its alternate name of Imperial Sojourn Palace (Miyuki Goten), that it was built in preparation for one of the Retired Emperor Gomizunoo's visits. It appears to have been constructed in about 1654–55 with some parts undergoing remodeling in about 1663. These dates, however, must remain conjectural. The completed complex combines elements of tea taste with courtly sensibility to produce a *sukiya shoin* country retreat perfect for learned and refined aristocrats.

Old Shoin

The Old Shoin, located atop a slight rise is the earliest surviving example of a nobleman's country villa (pl. 13). Its exterior differs from those of the structures behind it in that it has a white-plaster wall below the outside edge of its veranda where the others support their verandas with posts alone. Its exterior screens, too, are located at the inside edge of the veranda, whereas those of the other structures were redesigned in the mid-Edo period and are now at the veranda's outside edge, making for very little eave overhang. The eaves of the Old Shoin are the highest, with those of the Middle Shoin about thirty centimeters lower, and those of the New Palace about ten centimeters lower still.

One enters the Old Shoin via the Mikoshiyose (*genkan* entrance) at its north side, reached after passing along several rustic walks and through a variety of gates which set a mood of restful tranquility. Directly south of this is a *tatami* corridor, then a north and a south row of rooms. The most important of these are the Ni no Ma and the Ichi no Ma (pl. 148), both of which look east over a veranda to the pond. Beyond the veranda in front of the Ni no Ma is the famous Moon-viewing Platform, floored with bamboo (pl. 12). The row of rooms at the northwest of the Old Shoin have been redesigned, but were a servants' area and kitchen in the mid-Edo period.

These interior rooms are very simple, with a plain grill transom and no frieze rails. The Ichi no Ma, the most important room in the structure, has no ornamentation save a *tokonoma*, the post of which has unplaned corners. All other posts in the structure are square. In sum, the design is of the *sukiya shoin* type, but of a very early stage. The Old Shoin appears to have been used for informal meetings with guests.

Middle Shoin

Proceeding through the Hearth Room (Irori no Ma), one reaches the Middle Shoin, the floor of which is raised one step above that of the Old Shoin. The north half of the structure contains the San no Ma at the north and the Ichi no Ma and Ni no Ma to the south (pl. 149), all these bounded on the garden side by a *tatami* corridor. Projecting from this section to the south is the Instrument Room, where musical instruments were kept, and a bath area.

The Ichi no Ma contains a large *tokonoma* on the west wall and, at right angles to it at the north, a shelf alcove. The *tokonoma* painting, a subdued ink monochrome landscape, was done by Kanō Tan'yū, the premier painter of the day. The San no Ma also has a *tokonoma* but smaller in size. Despite the rather standard design of the *tokonoma* and shelves of the Ichi no Ma, the Middle Shoin is a more advanced form of *sukiya shoin* than the Old Shoin, making liberal use of posts with unplaned corners and also an interestingly shaped transom. The structure was apparently used as a living area.

New Palace

One step back from the Instrument Room is the New Palace, also of an irregular plan with the Ni no Ma leading into the Ichi no Ma at the southeast corner. Both rooms are bordered with a corridor interesting in that its inner half is *tatami* and its outer half polished, deep-grained wood with a brilliant luster (pl. 150). A railing separates the corridor from the exterior *shōji* screens. To the west, behind the main rooms, are sleeping and dressing rooms, indicating that the New Palace was used as a private

149. The Ichi no Ma viewed from
the Ni no Ma; Middle Shoin, Katsura
Detached Palace.

150. The southeast corner of the
Ichi no Ma veranda; New Palace,
Katsura Detached Palace.

151. The Imperial Dais of the Ichi no Ma; New Palace, Katsura Detached Palace.

space. More decorative than either the Old Shoin or the Middle Shoin, the New Palace shows the *sukiya shoin* style at its best.

The single most impressive element of the New Palace is the Imperial Dais (pl. 151), a three-mat *jōdan* section in the southwest corner of the Ichi no Ma. On its south side is a one-bay-wide *tsukeshoin*, with a motif in the shape of an arched keystone above the *shōji*. Next to it is a right-angled shelf design of great complexity. Known as Katsura Shelves (*katsura-dana*), they are counted among the three finest in Japan. The ink monochrome cabinet paintings it contains were painted by Tan'yū. Overhead is a lowered, coffered ceiling with black-lacquered runners. Many exotic woods are incorporated in this epitome of *sukiya shoin* styling.

Between the Ichi no Ma and the Ni no Ma (pl. 152), which also has a *tokonoma* with an oval cut-out on the side, is the famous Katsura transom, the insets of which are likened by some to the Sino-Japanese character for "moon" (月) and by others to that for the Buddhist swastika (卍, *manji*). The design is thus known as a "moon-character" or "*manji*-character" transom. The posts and frieze rails of both exhibit unplaned corners. There are also fine cabinets in the dressing room behind the Imperial Dais, these often called "Rear Katsura Shelving" because of their location. Another shelf of triangular shape, called the Imperial Sword Shelf, is in the Imperial Sleeping Chamber behind the Ni no Ma. These design elements underscore the pronounced *sukiya shoin* cast of the New Palace.

179

152. The Ichi no Ma viewed from
the Ni no Ma; New Palace, Katsura
Detached Palace.

SHUGAKU-IN DETACHED PALACE AND THE GUEST HALL OF THE MIDDLE VILLA

The Shugaku-in Detached Palace is situated on a spacious site on the lower slope of Mount Hiei (pl. 153). It is divided into three constituent complexes, and the view from the uppermost is one of the most splendid anywhere in the country, overlooking Kyoto to the west and mountains to the north, and insinuating these magnificent vistas into its own landscaping in the "borrowed scenery" (*shakkei*) technique. The garden seems to melt into the distance, giving the viewer a feeling of infinite expansiveness, the effect being quite different from that created by the controlled vistas of Katsura. The most important building on the site from the point of view of *sukiya shoin* architecture is the Guest Hall of the Middle Villa, and its shelf alcove is numbered among the three finest in Japan.

The builder of the Shugaku-in was the retired Emperor Gomizunoo (1596–1680), and he himself played a major role in its design. Partially completed in 1659, it served as a rural estate for the retired emperor to spend in peace the last years of a life marked by both cultural activity and political conflict. An accomplished poet and an expert

180

153. Aerial view of the Shugaku-in Detached Palace. The Lower Villa is at left, Upper Villa above it, and Middle Villa at right.

in flower arrangement, he was tutored in the courtly arts by his uncle, Prince Hachijō-no-miya Toshihito, who began the building of Katsura Detached Palace. Gomizunoo's consort, Tokugawa Kazuko (1607–78), was the daughter of the second Tokugawa shogun, Hidetada. Part of the land on which the Shugaku-in was built belonged to her. The union made the third Tokugawa shogun, Iemitsu, the brother-in-law of Gomizunoo and it was he who rebuilt the Ninomaru Palace of Nijō Castle in preparation for Gomizunoo's visit in 1626. The emperor's relations with the Tokugawa were thus tightly interwoven—indeed, they became for the emperor insupportably so, and he abdicated in 1629 in resentment of shogunal interference. His daughter by Tokugawa Kazuko thereupon came to the throne and he became the retired emperor (*jōkō*), moving to the Sentō Palace built by the shogunate for him and his consort, who took the name Tōfukumon'in. Located to the southeast of the Imperial Palace, this complex included both the Sentō Palace for the retired emperor and the Nyoin Palace for Tōfukumon'in. The Guest Hall of the Shugaku-in was originally part of the latter complex.

181

The Upper and Lower Villas

When first completed, the palace consisted of only two sections—a Lower Villa (Shimo no Chaya) and, located higher up the gently sloping foot of Mount Hiei, an Upper Villa (Kami no Chaya). The Shugaku-in site had for centuries been recognized for its scenic splendor, and several villas and temples were already located there when the Shugaku-in project was conceived. The third section, the Middle Villa (Naka no Chaya), was constructed somewhat later. It is there that the Guest Hall is located.

The visitor enters the Shugaku-in at the Lower Villa, which includes a garden with a pleasant stream and the Jugetsu-kan teahouse. This complex originally included a number of structures, but today only the Jugetsu-kan remains and this a nineteenth-century reconstruction. The original building served as a place for the emperor to rest before continuing uphill to the Upper Villa, and also for interviews with guests.

A short walk lined by terraced fields leads from the rear gate of the Lower Villa to the Upper Villa, by far the largest of the three palace complexes. It centers on the Yokuryū (Bathing Dragon) Pond, which was created by damming several streams (pl. 154). Ringed by white gravel paths, trimmed shrubbery, and magnificent trees, the pond includes two waterfalls, one of which the Otowa River was diverted to create.

Today two pavilions remain in the Upper Villa. One, the Rin'un-tei, was originally part of an earlier complex. The present structure is believed to date from the third decade of the nineteenth century (pl. 154). Named "Pavilion Next to the Clouds," it is the highest point in the Shugaku-in, and it is from here that the panorama of the Upper Villa landscape garden and surrounding mountains can best be viewed. The pleasant splashing of the highest of the Upper Villa's waterfalls, Otaki, can be heard close by. The second pavilion, the Kyūsui-tei, is located on the Middle Island (Nakano-shima) of the Yokuryū Pond. A simple structure with a square plan, it incorporates an L-shaped *jōdan* area with a cornice above, from which the Upper Garden can be seen.

The Middle Villa and the Guest Hall

The Middle Villa, reached by taking the southern fork in the path from the back gate of the Lower Villa, was not part of Gomizunoo's original conception, but rather begun about a decade after the completion in 1659 of the Upper and Lower Villas. It was originally built as the residence of another of Gomizunoo's daughters, Ake-no-miya Mitsuko (or Teruko). It thereafter became the Rinkyū-ji temple, and in 1886 was designated the Shugaku-in Middle Villa. It includes two main structures, the Rakushi-ken and, attached to its south corner, the Guest Hall, both located to the northeast of a spacious garden with a stream and pond. These structures were given to the imperial family by the Rinkyū-ji in 1886, the temple being relocated just to the east.

182

The Rakushi-ken, the oldest structure remaining in the Middle Villa, was built in about 1668 as part of Princess Mitsuko's residence. Its main rooms are a six-mat Ichi no Ma and an eight-mat anteroom, both of which face south overlooking the garden. Many of the rooms, such as a *shoin* and kitchens, were removed from the structure when the Rinkyū-ji was transferred to its present location. Its two main rooms are simply designed and conservatively decorated, in marked contrast to the Guest Hall appended to the south.

The Guest Hall
The Guest Hall is the most famous structure at the Shugaku-in and its ornamentation is the most luxurious. Originally an audience hall in Empress Tōfukumon'in's Nyoin Palace, it was constructed in 1677 after fire destroyed the previous structure. The empress died in the next year, though, and the retired emperor two years later, soon after which Princess Mitsuko became a nun to pray for the welfare of her father's spirit, her residence becoming the Rinkyū-ji. Two years later the Audience Hall was moved to the site. Though it was altered during the move, the present configuration gives an accurate impression of the building's original appearance (pl. 155). Its floor was lowered during the move, though, and the building was turned clockwise ninety degrees from its original orientation.

The plan of the Guest Hall is roughly square, with the twelve-mat Ichi no Ma and the ten-mat Ni no Ma composing the southwestern row. The ten-mat San no Ma is to the northeast of the Ni no Ma, the three main rooms of the structure thus having an L-shaped configuration. To the northeast of the Ichi no Ma is a devotional chamber that dates to after the 1682 move. *Tatami* corridors with verandas beyond border the southwest and northwest sides.

The main room of the structure, the Ichi no Ma, is decorated with a one-bay *tokonoma* (pl. 156) and a one-and-a-half-bay shelf alcove to its right, the latter being known as the Mist Shelves (*kasumi-dana*) and counted among the three finest shelves in Japan (pl. 157). The room is finished in the height of elegance. The *fusuma* and *tokonoma* are decorated with diamond-pattern wainscoting of blue and gold. Clouds of gold dust float above, which reflect light to opulent effect. Among these clouds are affixed square cards in a regular, zigzag arrangement, with the upper cards bearing poems and those below, pictures of the scenes to which the upper cards refer. The nail covers, in the shape of minutely detailed cloisonné flower carts, are made with such skill that they are now stored elsewhere for safekeeping, though the marks they left are still visible at the intersections of the posts and frieze rails. On the *tatami* corridors are wooden doors between the Ichi no Ma and Ni no Ma and between the Guest Hall and the Rakushi-ken, which are well known for their paintings of carp behind gold netting and floats used in the Gion Festival, one of Kyoto's main summer events.

The proportions of the wooden members of the Guest Hall are relatively thick and the posts are square cut with beveled corners, both these elements being characteristic of the standard *shoin* style. But the design of the shelves and the light-hearted subjects of the paintings are definite *sukiya*-style aspects. It is a different style of *sukiya* design, though, than that seen at Katsura, this bringing to mind the fact that whereas Katsura was a nobleman's villa, the Guest Hall was originally part of an imperial palace.

155. The Guest Hall of the Middle Villa, Shugaku-in
Detached Palace.

156. *Tokonoma* of the Ichi no Ma; Guest Hall. Middle Villa, Shugaku-in Detached Palace.

157. "Mist Shelves" of the Ichi no Ma; Guest Hall, Middle Villa, Shugaku-in Detached Palace.

At the base of the shelf alcove is an L-shaped cabinet with sliding panels decorated with elegant polychrome paintings of *yūzen* textiles and paddle-shaped cloisonné finger-pulls. Built into the corner above these is a triangular cabinet with polychrome designs. Above are five zelkova-wood shelves in an arrangement that seems to hang like mist, hence its name. The poem cards affixed to the back wall extol the beauties of the Shugaku-in scenery. All the decorative metal plaques are figured with the hollyhock crest of the Tokugawa, underscoring how strongly the shogunate wished to identify itself with the imperial family, for whom the palace was built.

THE JIKŌ-IN SHOIN

Situated on a gentle rise, the Jikō-in Shoin commands a broad and scenic view of the Yamato plain, the site of the first flowering of Japanese culture in the sixth and seventh centuries. The temple was begun by Katagiri Sadamasa (1605–73) for the repose of the spirit of his father, and the Shoin, built in 1663, is thought to have originally been an abbot's quarters. Today the Jikō-in includes two Important Cultural Properties—the Shoin and an attached tearoom built in 1671, both enjoyed for their tranquil beauty by Sadamasa in his last years.

Sadamasa is better known as Sekishū, after the Chinese-style name for the province of Iwami (part of present-day Shimane Prefecture) of which he was titular governor. He was also lord of the Koizumi fief in Yamato, in which the Jikō-in is located. A skilled designer, he was responsible for a number of construction projects, among them the garden at the Sentō Palace in Kyoto, built for the retired emperor Gosai (1637–85). Sadamasa is best remembered, however, as a superlative master of tea. He was tea instructor to the fourth Tokugawa shogun, Ietsuna (1641–80), as well as the author of several treatises on the tea ceremony. He was, furthermore, the originator of the Sekishū style of tea, still practiced in Japan today. A daimyo, but one who learned tea from an adherent of Rikyū's style, Sekishū's tea taste is characterized by the introduction of the simple and naturalistic *wabi* elements prized by Rikyū into the *shoin*-style tearooms used in the "daimyo tea" of Enshū and others. The Jikō-in Shoin expresses this philosophy in architectural terms, retaining *shoin* elements but incorporating them into a very simple overall design.

The Plan and Interior Elements

The Shoin was designed in such a way as to use to best advantage the surrounding scenery of the Yamato Plain. One enters the building via a large west *genkan* (pl. 158), then proceeds to the main room, the Jūsanjō no Ma (thirteen mats), which looks out over the gardens to the countryside beyond (pl. 159). As the east and south sides of the room provide the view, they are fit with *shōji* and verandas beyond. The verandas serve to unite the garden and the interior of the Jūsanjō no Ma, modulating the transition between the structure itself and the natural environment in which it is set. One post has been removed from the east side as well, so as not to obscure the scenery. The same consideration has been applied to the posts of the veranda eaves, which are spaced as far apart as structurally feasible. These low eaves above and mats below seem to form a frame for the Yamato landscape, and visually draw the distant mountains and the immediate garden into a single pictorial composition in the "borrowed scenery" (*shakkei*) technique.

The interior of the main room employs planed posts with chamfers taken on the edges and does not use frieze rails, thereby evoking a gentle *sukiya*-style appearance. In the northeast corner are located a *tokonoma* on the north wall and a *tsukeshoin* on

188

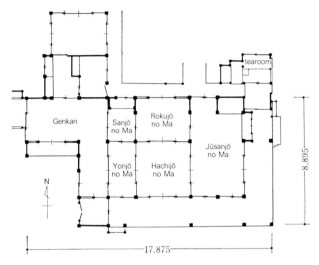

158. Plan of the Shoin, Jikō-in.

159. View east from the Jūsanjō no Ma, Jikō-in Shoin.   189

the east. Both are made very simply, reminding one of the style found in commoners' houses (*minka*). There are no staggered shelves, the single-bay space next to the *tokonoma* being instead fit with a *tatami* mat and sliding *fusuma* built in behind. When first built, this area may have been the location of a Buddhist altar. The general appearance of the Jūsanjō no Ma is one of simplicity, with no elaborate fixtures to detract from the scenic view.

West of the main room are the Hachijō no Ma (eight mats), which serves as the anteroom, and the Rokujō no Ma (six mats) probably used for relaxation. These rooms are located south and north, respectively. West again of these are the Yonjō no Ma (four mats) at the south and the Sanjō no Ma (three mats) at the north. The west end of the southern veranda can be closed off by an Envoy Gate (Chokushi-mon) with inward-opening, paneled, Chinese-style doors.

The Exterior
The hipped-and-gabled roof of the Shoin is thatched and is therefore more suggestive of a refined farmhouse than a temple building (pl. 160). The eaves are roofed with *sangawara* pantiles, which have a lighter appearance than the *hongawara* tiling with half-cylindrical ribbing used on large temples and palaces. The exterior combines well with the simplicity of the interior and harmonizes the structure with its natural surroundings. In its incorporation of farmhouse elements, the Jikō-in Shoin foreshadows the final stage of the *shoin* style, in which *shoin* elements are selectively incorporated into the homes of the lower classes. But the simplicity here goes hand in hand with great refinement, every element of the plan and location of this structure having been carefully considered in order to harmonize the building with its exterior environment as well as to profit from the surrounding view.

The Tearoom
At the northeast corner of the building is appended a tearoom with an area of two mats plus a *daime* (pl. 161), also an Important Cultural Property. Guests enter the room via the low-linteled door at the east and sit on the two guest mats immediately within, these lit by lattice windows at the south and east. Further back is the core of the room, the *daimegamae*, consisting of the sunken hearth, a *daime* mat behind it for the server, a center post of unique shape, and an attached clay wall left open at the bottom (*sodekabe*). Behind the server is the *tokonoma*, known by virtue of its positioning as a "server's *tokonoma*" (*teishu-doko*). This *tokonoma* location is not frequently seen in tearoom designs. The server's area, which can be entered by a separate southern door, is dimly lit in comparison to the mats for the guests, making the latter section seem open and airy. South of the guest mats is a two-mat anteroom which can be opened up or partitioned off by *fusuma* sliding screens.

161. Tearoom, Jikō-in.

The Shoin of the Shōgo-in

The *sukiya shoin* style reaches its final level of development at the Shoin of the Shōgo-in. Its main rooms exemplify the relaxed yet dignified atmosphere attainable through the mature introduction of teahouse elements into the *shoin* scheme.

The Shōgo-in is a major branch headquarters of the Jimon sect of Tendai Buddhism, the headquarters (Onjō-ji) of which includes the Kōjō-in and the Kangaku-in discussed in Chapter Three. After several relocations it was moved to its present site on the grounds of an old temple in 1676. The various structures, including the Hondō, Front Gate, Imperial Apartments, and the Shoin, were ready for use by 1680. It is not clear, however, when the Shoin itself was originally constructed, one theory being that it was moved to the Shōgo-in from the Imperial Palace. There are, though, no documents definitely proving this. The style of the structure, however, suggests a construction date near the end of the seventeenth century.

The Plan

The rooms of the Shoin are arranged in two rows, that to the north being for private use and that to the south for public purposes (pl. 162). One enters the structure through a *genkan* at the north, then can either proceed to the public area via the *tatami*-covered corridor (eight mats) which stretches the western length of the building, or proceed to the private section through the eight-mat Genkan Tsugi no Ma which contains a *tokonoma*. This north private row is composed of, from west to east, the Yonjō no Ma (four mats), the Rokujō no Ma (six mats), and the Hachijō no Ma (eight mats), the room sizes increasing as one proceeds further away from the *genkan*. A broad veranda borders the north and east sides of both the Genkan Tsugi no Ma and the Hachijō no Ma.

The south row includes the Ni no Ma anteroom (twelve mats) at the west and the Ichi no Ma main room (eight mats) at the east (pl. 163). The Ichi no Ma includes a *tokonoma* and staggered shelves on its far wall (the east) and a *tsukeshoin* at the south. Another shelf alcove and a *tokonoma* are located on the northern wall of the Ni no Ma. A broad veranda and an unfloored area under the eaves (*tsuchibisashi*) border on the west and south. In sum, the structure recalls the character of a subsidiary *shoin*, and was perhaps used as a residence.

The Interior of the Formal Rooms

The Ichi no Ma and the Ni no Ma are separated by *fusuma* and a simple, diamond-lattice transom (pl. 163). The *saobuchi* ceiling battens and embroidered *tatami* edges are set in both rooms parallel to the *tokonoma* and staggered shelves, which has the effect of leading the eye west to east down the length of the anteroom and into the Ichi no Ma, where the battens and mat lines run north and south, perpendicular to those of the anteroom, thus arresting visual progress.

192

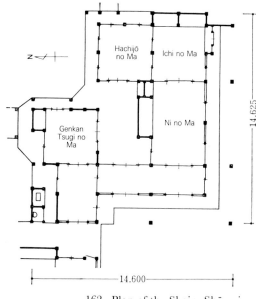

162. Plan of the Shoin, Shōgo-in.

The staggered shelves of the anteroom and the *tsukeshoin* of the Ichi no Ma are of old design and do not show the imagination of the *tokonoma* and shelves in the Ichi no Ma, which are masterpieces of *sukiya shoin* design (pl. 164). This Ichi no Ma shelf alcove is set at floor level, doing away with decorative molding (*kamachi*) and recessed floorboard (*kegomiita*). In this respect it is much like the staggered shelves of some modern Japanese homes. The tall lower cabinets take up over half this floor space, and are set in the corner diagonally below the upper cabinets, thus creating a balanced asymmetry. The shelves themselves are set at middle height, the left supported by a bracket in minutely carved arabesque openwork. A similar bracket visually supports the upper cabinets at the opposite side of the alcove. In a final novel touch, a lattice window has been fashioned into the upper part of the north alcove wall. This shelf alcove is one of the most advanced designs yet seen, novel in form and rich in detail. The *tokonoma* is equally developed, having, in the *sukiya* manner, a thin lintel and *tatami* floor, as well as a *tokonoma* post which has gone beyond the *menkawa* type with unplaned corners to a simpler, loglike design which is totally round save at the base. These elements show the Shōgo-in Shoin to have achieved a balanced blend of standard *shoin* and teahouse elements, the resultant *sukiya shoin* design being quite close in spirit to that of the traditional-style guest rooms of today.   193

194   164. *Tokonoma*, staggered shelves, and *tsukeshoin* of the Ichi no Ma, Shōgo-in Shoin.

THE SEISONKAKU

The Seisonkaku is a late-period pavilion of novel design located in Kanazawa City on the Sea of Japan. It was built in 1863 by the daimyo Maeda Nariyasu (1811–84) as a place of retirement for his mother, Shinryū'in. The Maeda family boasts an illustrious history. Its patriarch, Maeda Toshiie (1538–99), was an ally of Oda Nobunaga and later one of the five guardians of Toyotomi Hideyoshi's son, Hideyori. Toshiie's son, Toshinaga (1562–1614), fought on the side of Tokugawa Ieyasu at the decisive battle of Sekigahara in 1600 and controlled the Kaga fief from his castle in Kanazawa, and the fiefs of Noto and Echizen besides, amassing vast wealth. For the next two and a half centuries the Maeda controlled their immense holdings from Kanazawa, Shinryū'in being widow of the twelfth generation head of the family, Maeda Narihiro, father of Nariyasu.

The Seisonkaku was thus one of the final grand buildings to be built under Japan's feudal system, being constructed a decade after Commodore Perry first arrived and only five years before the Meiji Restoration ushered Japan into the modern age. It was built on the site of the old Takezawa Palace, the present Front Gate and retainers' apartments (*nagaya*) remaining from that complex. The Seisonkaku itself was the central building of the Tatsumi Shinden (literally, "New Palace of the Southeast") which was constructed in 1863. Shinryū'in died in 1870, and four years later the grounds were renamed the Kenroku Park, today one of the most famous public parks in Japan. The name Seisonkaku was given to Shinryū'in's apartments at this time.

The Plan and Interior
The complex design of the Seisonkaku reflects the wealth of the Maeda family and the high status of its resident, Shinryū'in. As suggested by the suffix *kaku*, meaning "pavilion," the building is of two-story design. On the ground floor, the formal and informal public areas, divided by a corridor, are at the northeast, and four main private rooms are at the southwest. A tearoom (the Seikō-ken) and the Seikō Shoin room beside it are included as well at the north corner. At the Seisonkaku, therefore, all the major spaces are again consolidated under one roof. In this, the building differs from the *shoin* style of Nijō Castle which is composed of several separate structures, each assigned one function. The second floor appears to have been used for special meetings with guests.

The most formal room of the mansion is the Ekken no Ma audience hall, bordered on the southeast and northwest by *tatami*-covered corridors (pl. 165). An anteroom (Tsugi no Ma) leads into the Ekken no Ma from the southwest, and the two rooms are divided by a detailed transom with carved openwork of birds amidst flowering branches. All the four interior fixtures of the standard *shoin* are included in the audience hall in the prescribed locations, with *tokonoma* and staggered shelves on the far wall, *tsukeshoin* on the wall nearest the exterior, and the *chōdaigamae* across from it

195

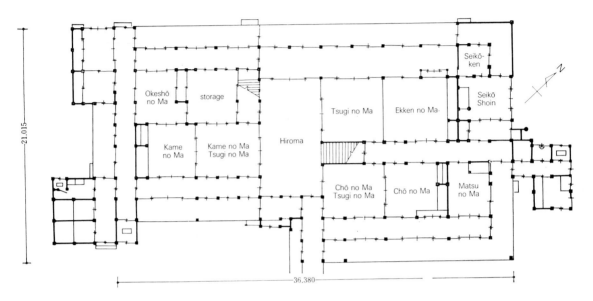

165. Plan of the first floor of the Seisonkaku.

opening into the interior central corridor (pl. 166). The *chōdaigamae* is interesting in its incorporation of lower runners which are higher on the wall than is usually seen. Appropriate to the formality of the room, the ceiling is coved and coffered.

Across the central corridor is the Chō no Ma (Butterfly Room) and coupled anteroom, the Chō no Ma Tsugi no Ma. The spaces function as a *goza no ma*, being used for daily affairs and relaxed interviews. Its less formal nature is at once clearly seen by comparison to the Ekken no Ma. As in the case of the Ekken no Ma, the *tokonoma* and staggered shelves are on the far wall, with the *tokonoma* on the outer side abutting at right angles with a *tsukeshoin*-like desk on the veranda wall (pl. 167). But this *tokonoma* is much smaller, and the writing space is not a projecting *tsukeshoin*, but rather a flat *tsukeshoin* with a simple *shōji* screen wall and a writing surface projecting into the room, here set with small sliding *fusuma* beneath the writing shelf. The *tsukeshoin* is one and a half bays in width and greatly illuminates the room. The shelves, too, are more complex and innovative than those of the Ekken no Ma and are quite light and functional.

The Matsu no Ma (Pine Room) in the east corner behind the Chō no Ma is one step further relaxed, its ornament restricted to a *tatami*-floored *tokonoma* with severed *tokonoma* post (*tokobashira*) and a very abbreviated *hirashoin* without a writing surface but inset with glass painted with pictures of birds (pl. 168). It is bordered, as is the Chō no Ma, by a corridor and a veranda.

196

166. Ekken no Ma, Seisonkaku.

167. Chō no Ma, Seisonkaku.　197

The private half of the first floor, at the southwest, is separated from the northeast public area by the Hiroma central room. Southwest of this is the Kame no Ma Tsugi no Ma (anteroom) and then the Kame no Ma (Tortoise Room). The Kame no Ma (twelve-and-a-half mats) served as the sleeping area and includes a *tokonoma* and staggered shelves. Beside these rooms is the Okeshō no Ma (Dressing Room) and a storage space. Both rows of rooms are bordered on their outer sides by corridors and outer verandas. At the far west corner are two small rooms for worship, and in the corner at the east the bath and toilet areas.

The second floor, entered via stairs leading from the Hiroma, is located above the Ekken no Ma and its anteroom. It is composed of two sections, the southwest half made up of three minor spaces, and the northeast, of three lavish ones. These latter rooms are the Etchū no Ma, the Ajiro no Ma, and the Gunjō no Ma. The Etchū no Ma (not illustrated) includes such teahouse elements as a polished, unplaned *tokonoma* post (*tokobashira*) and a round, wattled window. The room serves as the entry to both the Ajiro no Ma and to the main room of the second floor, the Gunjō no Ma (Ultramarine Room), so named because of its dazzling and intense coloration (pl. 169). It is composed of a nine-mat space and a smaller three-mat area to which is added a *jōdan* section (pl. 170). On two sides are verandas overlooking a garden. On the south wall of its nine-mat space is located a *murodoko*, a deep *tokonoma* with arched lintel (not illustrated), and at the east corner is a shelf alcove with tall lower cabinets. Northeast of this main room is the three-mat-plus-*jōdan* area, separated from the former space by a transom inset with *shōji*. The room appears to have been for the personal use of Shinryū'in and for her informal visits with guests, and as such has a markedly different character from the formal rooms on the first floor below.

The Seisonkaku is, in sum, a delightful and unique structure, incorporating in one building strict *shoin*, relaxed *shoin*, and *sukiya shoin* styles. There is no other extant structure which includes such complexity and variation under one roof. Its imaginative design reflects the character of late Edo architecture and its richness recalls the life style of the last generations of the feudal ruling class.

168. *Tokonoma* of the Matsu no Ma, Seisonkaku.

169. Gunjō no Ma, Seisonkaku.
This *sukiya*-style room breaks with the traditional *shoin* configuration, having a very free arrangement of *tokonoma*, staggered shelves, and writing desk. This imaginative design lends the room a clear *sukiya* quality, which is enhanced by the *menkawa* posts with unplaned corners. The room takes its name from its startling ultramarine (*gunjō*) coloration.

170. *Jōdan* of the Gunjō no Ma, Seisonkaku.
In place of a *tsukeshoin* alcove that projects into a veranda, the *jōdan* of the Gunjō no Ma uses for a writing area a simple plank (*hiradana*) appended to a flat wall inset with an ogee-arched window. The writing surface is juxtaposed to a narrow shelf alcove which is, in turn, set into a *tatami*-covered *tokonoma*.

6

THE MINKA SHOIN

As we have seen, the *shoin* style developed from the late Muromachi period as the residential style of the upper classes—the high-level military, the court aristocracy, and the affluent clergy. Elements of the style later came, however, to be adopted as well by the wealthier members of the lower classes for use in their best formal reception rooms. These houses of the lower classes are known as *minka*, a broad term referring both to urban residences (*machiya*) and rural farm houses (*nōka*) whose owners were not of the highest strata of society. It applies to the barest homes of the poorest farmers as well as to the residences of the lower-level samurai, inns for traveling daimyo and government officials, and the mansions of the wealthy merchants of the cities and towns whose houses often rivaled those of their warrior class rulers but whose commoner status under the fixed social hierarchy defined by the government was below even that of farmers and artisans.

Of the *minka* in existence today, the earliest is thought to date from about the end of the Muromachi period (1333–1567). The earliest example for which we have a precise date, however, is the Kuriyama Residence in Gojō, Nara Prefecture, which has a ridgepole certificate inscribed with the year 1607.

Perhaps because the *minka* were the residences of the lower classes, they were in general overlooked as objects of artistic worth until after the Second World War. But with the rise of interest in social history and the decline in the number of surviving *minka*, concern has recently increased markedly and a number have come to be designated Important Cultural Properties. As *minka* gained increasing attention, they were discovered to retain elements of earlier architectural styles. It was realized that, viewed as a group, they provide glimpses of the entire history of Japanese domestic architecture as a result of traditional elements and techniques having been handed down unchanged through the ages and incorporated in the buildings of new generations as they were in those of the old. This continual respect for and incorporation of traditional elements is a major factor in all Japanese domestic architecture.

The plan of the Kuriyama Residence provides a good example of this respect for earlier design elements. The town house of wealthy merchants, the residence is quite large, with thick plaster walls and a hipped-and-gabled roof with heavy temple-style *hongawara* tiling. The plan is typical of large-scale town houses, with a hard-packed earthen-floor area at one side and on the other side a raised, plank-floored section with two rows of three rooms each (pl. 171). Although the building was extensively remodeled in later years, it is sure that the middle room in the rear row of the raised section originally had wooden panels on three sides and a *chōdaigamae*. Thus the seventeenth-century Kuriyama Residence included the same type of enclosed sleeping area used in the *shinden* style in the Heian period. It will be interesting to see what other early elements appear when a full dismantling for repairs is carried out.

This retention of traditional elements is a source of great interest and appeal, for it has contributed to the continuation of regional differences in *minka* styles, differences which were introduced to Westerners as early as 1886 in Edward Morse's *Japanese Homes and Their Surroundings*. These differences initially developed in response to the varying climates and customs in various parts of the country. The *gasshō* style, used in Shirakawa, Gifu Prefecture, and Gokayama in Toyama, has a steep-pitched roof with three floors to accommodate the silkworm industry of the region. In like manner, the *chūmon* style, used in the "snow country" on the northern coast of the Sea of Japan, includes the entrance, stables, and toilet in an ell projecting at right angles from the house proper. This ensures constant access to those sections even in the deepest snows, forms a protective porch for the entry area, and stabilizes the high roof used to keep snow accumulation on it to a minimum.

But despite the regional differences exhibited by *minka*, the division of the floor area into an earthen-floor section and an area with a raised and boarded floor seems a general trait. The earthen-floored area, often called the *doma* or *niwa*, was used usually for cooking, storage, and as a sleeping area for servants. Above it stretch the huge bowed and twisted beams that support the weight of the roof. The area with the raised wood floor, often covered in full or in part by *tatami* mats, is used for daily living. This division applies to town houses and farm houses alike, though the area allotted to each varies from house to house.

But the *minka* are not static stylistically, despite the constant reuse of traditional techniques. The most important case in point is the gradual incorporation by the *minka* of *shoin* elements from warrior mansions, a development that became widespread by the middle of the Edo period but which had begun much earlier. These *shoin* elements, including the formal reception room and its internal elements such as the *tokonoma*, staggered shelves, *tsukeshoin*, frieze rails, ceilings, and decorated *fusuma*, and the separate gatehouse and formal entryway (*genkan*), were normally forbidden to the classes below that of the samurai. Village headmen, however, although of the farmer class, were allowed the privilege of constructing a formal reception room, as they functioned as local officials for the Tokugawa government and, in this capacity, were required to entertain visiting higher officials for whom protocol required a *shoin* room. Their houses functioned in many cases rather like country town halls—decrees were

203

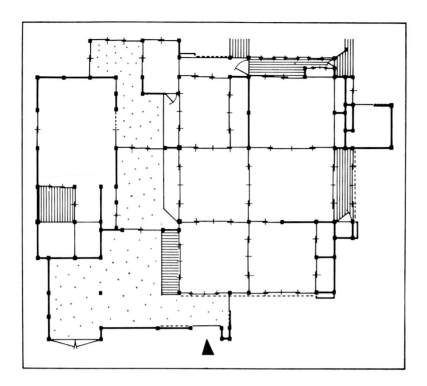

171. Plan of the Kuriyama Residence.

posted there, taxes in kind were stored within, and assemblies and trials were carried out in the yard. There were instances, in fact, where the formal reception room would be built onto the headman's house at village expense. Occasionally the formal area was built as a separate structure, preserving the *shoin* tradition seen at Nijō Castle of locating spaces of separate function under separate roofs.

As time passed, however, some merchants, who by law were at the bottom of the Tokugawa social hierarchy, began amassing considerable wealth and incorporating *shoin* elements into their houses as well, upsetting the minutely balanced social system maintained by the government. The Tokugawa, consequently, were continually at pains to limit such building through sumptuary laws. These complex laws covered not only homes, but stipulated details such as what clothing types were allowed which classes. Building restrictions were placed not only on the reception room elements, but covered the size of the house, length of the roof beam, number of ridge ornaments, and type of roofing material, to mention only a few. Theoretically it was possible to deduce the subdivision of the farming class to which any farmer belonged by examining the house in which he lived. In practice, however, these sumptuary laws were not enforced equally throughout the country, and homes in the Kyoto, Nara, and Osaka areas tended to be more luxurious than those nearer Edo, the seat of the government.

Furthermore, the right to incorporate *shoin* elements in one's house could be purchased by wealthy members of the classes not ordinarily entitled to them. As time passed, it became increasingly difficult for the government to effectively force those with the financial means from incorporating architectural symbols of the upper class into their own residences.

The houses dealt with in this chapter all belonged to wealthy members of the lower classes, and all incorporate *shoin* style elements in varying degree. They are thus much larger and ornate than typical *minka*. All date most likely to the Edo period and all are Important Cultural Properties. It is from these houses that the custom of decorating the best room in a residence with *shoin* elements passed into the traditional-style Japanese houses of today.

THE IMANISHI RESIDENCE

Save for the Kuriyama Residence mentioned earlier, the mansion of the Imanishi family is the oldest *minka* to which an exact and reliable date can be affixed, the extant ridgepole certificate giving the date of construction as 1650. The head of the Imanishi family was one of the headmen who oversaw town business. The house, a town-house type of *minka*, is located in Imai-chō, a small ward established in the century of civil war (1467–1568). This ward was built around the Jōdo Shinshū temple of Shōnen-ji by adherents of that sect and was, like the famous port city of Sakai near Osaka, a self-governing entity. Walls and a moat were constructed to preserve the town's autonomy, and roads were constructed in such a manner as to afford no long views and to obstruct the movements of large numbers of men and horses, thus allowing for better defense. As headmen, the Imanishi were of considerable importance, and their mansion has been likened to a castle because of its two-story-tall white walls, thick lattice windows, and heavy roof covered with *hongawara* temple-style tile (pl. 172). The walls are particularly striking and are representative of the "broad-wall style" (*ōkabe-zukuri*) in which the posts are covered over with plaster so as to create an expansive and undifferentiated white wall surface. In this and other broad-wall style *minka*, though, the facade of the first floor is of the regular *shinkabe* type, with posts left visible. The roof design is very complex, being a good example of the *yatsumune-zukuri*, meaning literally "eight-ridge style" but descriptive in general of complicated roof and gable configurations influenced by castle architecture.

As opposed to the Kuriyama house, which has yet to be thoroughly investigated, the Imanishi mansion has been completely dismantled for repairs and was, on the basis of a minute inspection of the constituent parts carried out at that time, completely restored to its original configuration (pl. 173). The ground floor plan of the mansion is similar to that of most *minka*, with one half being a large earthen-floored space (*doma*) with huge roof beams above, and the other a raised-floor section with two rows of rooms running back from the road in front. One enters the mansion via the "great

172. Exterior of the Imanishi Residence.

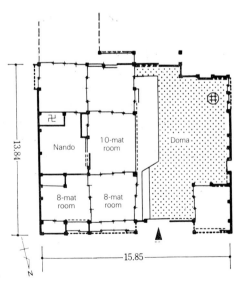

173. Plan of the Imanishi Residence.

174. Living area viewed from the *doma*, Imanishi Residence.

door" to the earthen-floored area, then turns left and steps up to the pair of eight-mat rooms which flank the street (pl. 174). Both are known as the *mise* or "shop" where business transactions took place. The *mise* farthest from the *doma* functions as the formal parlor and includes a *tokonoma*, reflective of the high status of the master. To the rear of the two *mise* are a pair of ten-mat rooms, the one close to the *doma* serving as a living area and the further one as the sleeping and storage space (*nando*). As in the Kuriyama Residence, this sleeping room is fit with *chōdaigamae*. An eight-mat kitchen/eating area and, further back, an eight-mat altar room with appended four-mat, then eight-mat rooms, completes the ground floor plan.

The most outstanding feature of the second floor is the presence of a second *tokonoma*. This *tokonoma*, together with that of the guest room, proves that *tokonoma* were being included in *minka* by at least the early Edo period, and that the *tokonoma* was viewed, then as now, as the single most important element of the formal room.

THE YOSHIMURA RESIDENCE

The Yoshimura Residence is one of the finest farmhouse-type *minka* extant. It is famous in particular for its superb facade (pl. 176), the design of which is created by the asymmetrical yet balanced crisscrossing of posts and tie beams with interspersed lattices and verandas. This variegation contrasts with the solidity and quietude of the tile eaves and the thatched roof above. The elegance born here of the masterly combination of simple constituent elements makes the Yoshimura Residence one of the most aesthetically pleasing *minka* to be seen today.

175. Ichi no Ma of the Yoshimura Residence.
The guest section of the Yoshimura Residence
includes the main Ichi no Ma and an anteroom,
the Ni no Ma. The former includes a *tokonoma*
and *tsukeshoin*. The posts with unplaned edges,
the thin *tokonoma* lintel, and the ogee-arched
window of the *tsukeshoin* are all elements that
developed relatively late, suggesting the guest
section was probably built after the seventeenth
century.

176. South facade of the Yoshimura Residence.

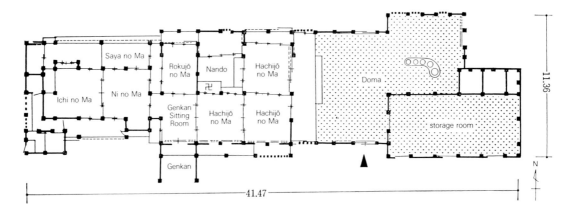

177. Plan of the Yoshimura Residence.

The size and refinement of the Yoshimura Residence is appropriate to the important position of its past owners, wealthy farmers who served as general supervisors (*ōjōya*) over the headmen of the various towns in the district. They were, in this capacity, granted the sword-carrying privilege usually reserved for members of the warrior class. The date in which their house was constructed is not clear. It may be, in fact, that different sections were built at different times. The middle portion, thought to be the oldest, probably dates from the beginning of the Edo period.

The plan of the residence is oriented east to west and is quite narrow (pl. 177). It consists of, from east to west, an earthen-floored *doma* with storage area, a central six-room living section, and three rooms for formal reception purposes. These divisions are reflected in the roof design, in which the *doma* and storage area is covered by a gently sloping tile roof with chimney, and the central section is roofed with a steeper-sloped thatched roof with tiled eaves of a gentler slope below. This latter roof configuration is frequently found in the Yamato, Kawachi, and Iga regions of Japan (the northern part of the Kii Peninsula) and is consequently known as a "Yamato roof" (*yamatomune*), or as the "high wall style" (*takahei-zukuri*), so named because of its steep, stuccoed gables.

The earthen-floored *doma* is a vast single space with massive soot-blackened beams above, atop which rests a bamboo ceiling (*sunoko tenjō*). The storage room, which includes a second floor for servants, may be a later addition. One particularly novel element of the *doma* space is the tiny room suspended above the raised floor at the west wall (pl. 178). This room too was used for servants, who entered it by climbing the ladder fashioned of crescent-shaped indentations in the wall beneath.

178. *Doma* of the Yoshimura Residence.

The central section of the house is composed of six rooms in a fairly regular two-row design (pl. 177). The center room of the rear row is a plank-floored *nando*. The seven-mat area at the southwest of the six-room central group is the Genkan Sitting Room, and the Genkan formal entryway is appended to it at the south. It is from these two rooms that high-ranking visitors would proceed into the west *shoin*-style guest wing. Many upper-class *minka* complexes, such as those of the Naka and Furui families discussed further on, include a separate structure, connected to the main dwelling via corridors, to house the *shoin* rooms. In the Yoshimura house, however, the *shoin* section is directly juxtaposed to the living area. The guest wing is, however, distinctly separated visually by its roof design, which is tiled and more gently sloped than the thatched roof over the house's central section.

The west guest wing is composed of an eight-mat Ni no Ma anteroom and, beyond it to the west, a nine-mat Ichi no Ma. North of the Ni no Ma is a four-mat Scabbard Room (Saya no Ma), and the Ni no Ma anteroom itself is equipped with a one-mat space for preparing tea.

The Ichi no Ma is a clear example of *shoin* elements being adopted into the *minka*, as it is ornamented with a *tokonoma* adjacent to it on the north wall (pl. 175). This *tsukeshoin* is set in standard position on the veranda side, this side being the main facade of the guest section and constructed so as to face out over a garden. These two rooms, clearly inspired by the *shoin* style, bear witness to the confluence of that style with that of the *minka*.

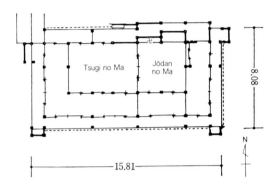

179. Plan of the Shoin, Furui Residence.

THE SHOIN OF THE FURUI RESIDENCE

According to a plan dated 1835, the residence of the Furui family was massive and included a main house, storehouses, barns, and even an archery range and riding ground. Today, however, the only preserved portion is the two-room *shoin* area located at the far end of the original complex. These rooms are, however, quite elegant and bear witness to the importance of the Furui family, one of the wealthiest in the region. The date of construction is not certain, but probably falls near the middle of the seventeenth century. The house may even antedate that of the Yoshimura family.

The Shoin (pl. 179) is comprised of a Jōdan no Ma (eight mats) to the east and, a shallow step below it to the west, a Tsugi no Ma anteroom (twelve mats). A hip roof of thatch covers the structure and enclosed *tatami* corridors and outer wooden verandas flank all sides save the north.

Included in the Jōdan no Ma are *tokonoma*, staggered shelves, and a *tsukeshoin*, which implies that the room was used for receiving visitors of high rank (pl. 180). This sophistication is matched by the ceiling which is constructed in the *sarubō* style, a very high quality design which calls for the corners of the battens (*saobuchi*) to be chamfered rather than left square. The *tokonoma*, at the east side of the north wall, has a lintel thicker than that of the Yoshimura house, which may indicate an earlier date of construction. The shelves are built in the very formal *seirō-dana* design with a raised central section, and upper cupboards are included as well. The *tsukeshoin*, in its orthodox position on the veranda wall, is of quite simple style. The placement of these interior fixtures is of older fashion than that seen in the Yoshimura Jōdan no Ma, and the same is true for the treatment of the posts. The *menkawa* style, with planed but rough edges, is used for the wall posts, but the posts in the corners are of the square type.

180. *Tokonoma* and staggered shelves of the Jōdan no Ma, Furui Residence.

In sum, although the Furui Residence belongs to the *minka* category, these two rooms are clearly of a sophisticated *shoin* style lineage and rival in elegance many of the homes of warriors in the early Edo period.

The Naka Residence

The Naka Residence is located in Kumatori-chō, the same ward in which the Furui family house is situated. Both residential complexes included separate sections for daily living and formal audiences, but whereas the section remaining of the Furui Residence is part of the visitor section, that surviving from the Naka house was for daily activities. Mentally combining the two thus gives a good idea of what a full-scale upper-class *minka* dwelling looked like in this locale.

As reflected in the scale of their residences, the Naka and the Furui were among the most important of the commoner families in the region. The Naka, in fact, are said to have descended from samurai of the medieval period. Just as the roofs of the Nino-maru Palace served to awe those beyond the castle walls, so does the roof of the Naka house impress upon the viewer the importance of those living within. It has a hipped-and-gabled thatched design, with *hongawara* tiling on the eaves. This two-part design, with different slopes and two types of roofing, resembles a warrior's helmet with a neckpiece (*shikoro*) and is consequently referred to as *shikoro* roofing. The name is also applied to roofs entirely of thatch with two-part slopes or with two thatching techniques. The grandest element, though, of the Naka Residence roof is the huge tri-comma circular carving on the gable. Known as a *mitsudomoe*, it may have functioned as a charm to protect the house from conflagration.

The room arrangement of the Naka home is quite complicated, and by virtue of   213

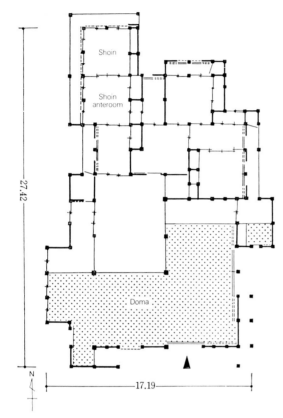

Shoin

Shoin anteroom

Doma

27.42

17.19

N

181. Plan of the Naka Residence.

an extant old plan it is clear that the house was considerably rearranged in later years. The only rooms, in fact, which retain their early configuration are the two *shoin*-type rooms in the very back of the structure. The dates of the house are unclear, and although the thick proportions of the columns suggest a date as early as the Keichō period (1596–1615), this is at best only speculation.

The plan of the house today can be divided roughly in half, with the *doma* area to the south and living area to the north (pl. 181). The two formal eight-mat *shoin* spaces are located in the northwest corner. The original room layout between the entrance and rearmost *shoin* spaces was even more complex than it is today, which indicates that the *shoin* rooms were not used for interviews but rather as the living section for the master. Were these rooms for audiences with guests, the progression from the entrance would no doubt have been less complicated.

The two *shoin* style rooms are bordered by wooden verandas on the north and west sides, beyond which is a garden. At the east end of the north veranda used to be appended bath and toilet facilities. The closer of the two rooms to the main entrance of the house serves as the anteroom. Beyond it is the more important of the spaces, ornamented with a *tokonoma* and staggered shelves on the east wall with the *tokonoma* in the standard location nearer the veranda and flanked by a *hirashoin* on the north wall. The lintel of the *tokonoma* is of a thin, late style, as it is at the Yoshimura Residence, and the *tokonoma* post (*tokobashira*) is not of the *menkawa* type with unplaned corners, but is rather an unplaned log, this even more naturalistic than the *menkawa* type. The shelves have an innovative design incorporating a small cabinet with *fusuma* panels between the two shelf levels. The floor boarding beneath them has disposed altogether with the decorative molding and is level with the *tatami*. All these design factors are of quite advanced style, and indicate the *tokonoma* and staggered shelves may have been rebuilt at a later date. Even so, these two rooms indicate that elements of the *shoin* style were not only adopted into the guest rooms of *minka* homes, but could also be used in the private area of a residence.

THE WATANABE RESIDENCE

The Watanabe family established itself in Niigata, a northern prefecture of abundant snowfall, in the mid-seventeenth century, and amassed a considerable fortune as *sake* brewers. They served at one time in the elevated post of district magistrate and were the supervisory headmen of their locality. This social position was elevated enough to merit the sword-bearing privilege usually reserved for those of the warrior class. The present Watanabe mansion was constructed in 1788 after fire destroyed their previous residence.

Built along a broad street and provided with a moat, the residence presents to the passer-by a beautifully conceived two-story facade of long, unbroken eaves with rhythmically placed projecting latticework beneath (pl. 182). Surmounting the central section of the facade is the gable of the gently sloped shingled roof, topped at the ridge with a "crow perch" (*karasudomari*) ornament. Atop the roof rest hundreds of flat stones, their weight securing the wooden shingles beneath. The gently sloped roof is thought to have been developed as one way to deal with the heavy snows of the region. The shallow slope keeps the accumulated snow and ice from crashing off all at once.

Two main entrances face the street (pl. 183)—the western one a *genkan* for those of elevated station such as the lord of the Yonezawa fief, and the eastern one a huge double door embellished with heavy iron patera-shaped nail-concealers. This entrance was for the use of the tenant farmers when they brought in their annual tax in rice. This double door leads into the broad and deep earthen-floored eastern half of the mansion, called here the *niwa*, an alternate word for *doma*. Bordering the *niwa* on the west is a long row of rooms with raised floors of *tatami* or wood and, as in the 215

182. South facade of the Watanabe Residence.

niwa, exposed beams and no ceilings. It was in this row of rooms that the daily life of the household took place. This row is composed of a six-mat corridorlike space directly behind the central lattice on the facade and then a Hiroma behind it. The Hiroma, also known as the Kanjō no Ma or Accounting Room, was used as a general office space and reception area. Behind this is the Tearoom, in this case a sixteen-mat area in which visiting farmers and tradespeople were given hospitality. The *niwa* leads naturally to this room as there is no wall separating the two, only a difference in floor height. Back further still from the facade is the wood-floored Middle Tearoom (six mats) and, behind it, the kitchens. These two rooms also open directly on to the *niwa*, with no intervening walls. West of the Middle Tearoom–kitchen area is the Nando no Ma, a spacious room which the family used as a living space. It is provided with a *tokonoma* and staggered shelves on the north wall. Above this space on the second floor is a reception room with *tokonoma* and staggered shelves used as a secondary formal space.

The rooms for receiving important guests are found to the west of the *genkan* entrance, which itself is furnished with a *tokonoma* of impressive size. One first passes through the Ni no Ma anteroom which is ornamented with a *tokonoma*. This anteroom is flanked at the south by a six-mat corridorlike space and projecting lattice arrange-

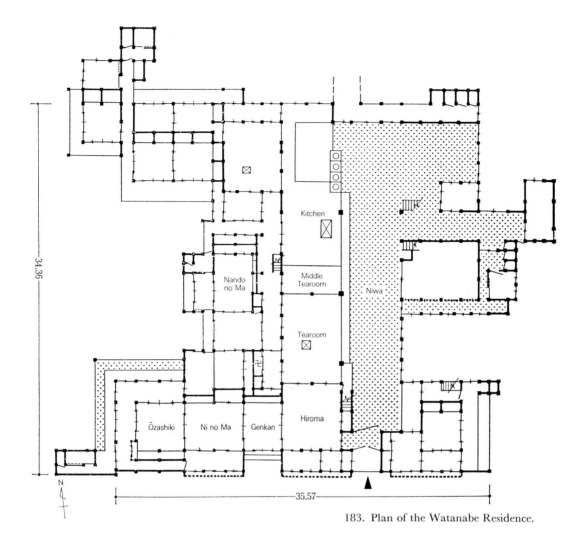

In the plan labels: Kitchen, Nando no Ma, Middle Tearoom, Niwa, Tearoom, Ōzashiki, Ni no Ma, Genkan, Hiroma

34.36

35.57

N

ment much like that to the south of the Hiroma. West of the Ni no Ma, projecting by itself beyond the main building block, is the Ōzashiki formal reception room, bordered on the west and north sides by *tatami* corridors, outer wooden verandas, and unfloored areas under the broad eaves. This arrangement provides for a most elegant view of a garden famed for its beauty and sophistication. Connected at the west are a bath house and toilet. The Ōzashiki itself includes a *tokonoma* and staggered shelves arranged west and east on the south wall (pl. 184). A *tsukeshoin* flanks the *tokonoma* on the west wall.

The design of these interior fixtures is quite innovative. The strict *shoin* style is reflected in the use of wall paper on the *tokonoma* and shelf alcove wall, but the interesting shelf configuration and central *tokonoma* post (*tokobashira*) with *menkawa* unplaned corners show instead a relaxed *sukiya* design. By the late eighteenth century, then, it is clear from the Watanabe Residence that a well-established standard *shoin* scheme with *tokonoma*, staggered shelves, and *tsukeshoin* in the most formal room and large *tokonoma* in the *genkan* had reached the upper-level *minka*-type houses in even the remote northern provinces. It shows further that *sukiya*-style elements, marked by inventive and naturalistic design, were used in this area by this time as well.

217

184. *Tokonoma* and staggered shelves of the Ōzashiki, Watanabe Residence.

THE SASAGAWA RESIDENCE

Located on a site nearly five acres in size, the Sasagawa Residence is, along with that of the Watanabe, one of the most magnificent *minka* in northern Japan. Its owners were supervisory headmen under the direction of the Murakami fief, and oversaw the administration of fifteen surrounding villages. The present residence, resplendent with nine-hundred-year-old cedars and a moat, dates to 1826 according to an extant ridgepole certificate, having been rebuilt after fire destroyed much of the previous residence.

After passing beneath the Front Gate, one of the structures that survived the 1826 fire, the visitor faces the east side of the Outer Zashiki structure, which includes the business area and formal *shoin* reception rooms of the mansion. The walkway divides past the gate, stretches across the entry courtyard, and then the north leg divides again, giving a choice of three entrances for the visitor to choose according to the level of his social station and the nature of his visit. The entrance at the north is the general entrance leading into the earthen-floored *doma* space (pl. 185). As typically the case for an overseer's mansion, it was here that the tenant farmers brought in their yearly taxes in kind to be recorded and stored. Above, spanning the dimly lit *doma*, are massive, twisted roof beams, used in some strategic points in pairs to provide reinforcement against the tons of snow that accumulate in the winter months on the roof above.

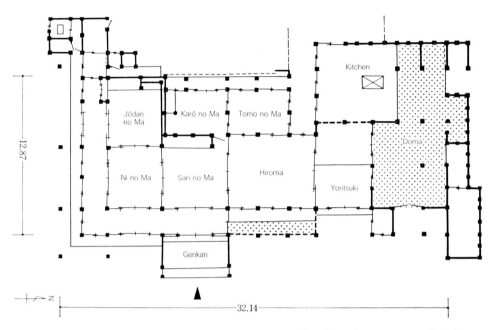

185. Plan of the Sasagawa Residence.

The middle entry leads into an area called the Yoritsuki where routine business was carried out. This area is floored half in planks and half in *tatami* and borders on the *doma* at the north, from which it can be separated by sliding partitions. Behind it is the kitchen, which then connects to a corridor leading to the living section of the mansion, a separate building to the west of the Outer Zashiki structure. Bordering on the Yoritsuki at the south is the Hiroma, a twenty-eight-mat room for office work or interviews. The wooden sliding partitions and exposed beams above place this room squarely in the farmhouse (*nōka*) tradition and contrast with the papered *fusuma* and hung ceilings of the more formal *shoin*-style rooms to the south.

When calling on the Sasagawa family, the lord of the Murakami fief or other high-ranking visitors would choose the southernmost walkway from the Front Gate, which leads to the formal *genkan* area, this clearly indicated by a huge, gently arched entry-way roof. This *genkan* opens into the San no Ma. The visitor, upon entering, faces a huge, two-and-a-half-bay *tokonoma* papered a dramatic indigo. The inclusion of a *tokonoma* reminds one of the Watanabe Residence. Behind the San no Ma is the ten-mat Karō no Ma, with rebuilt *tokonoma* and staggered shelves. This room is entered, however, via the ten-mat Tomo no Ma bordering it at the north and located behind the Hiroma. Next to the San no Ma at the south end of the residence are the formal rooms—the Ni no Ma anteroom at the front and the Jōdan no Ma at the rear. Both

219

186. Jōdan no Ma viewed from the Ni no Ma, Sasagawa Residence.

rooms are bordered with *tatami* corridors and lower wood verandas and, beyond this, an unfloored area. At the far west end of these verandas are located bath and toilet rooms. Despite its name, the Jōdan no Ma does not include a *jōdan* area, being instead on the same level as the anteroom. However, the decorative elements specified for a formal *shoin* room are here in evidence, with *tokonoma* and staggered shelves located south and north on the west wall (pl. 186).

The south side of the *tokonoma* abuts on a *tsukeshoin* which projects into the southern veranda. A polished, unplaned post serves as the *tokonoma* post (*tokobashira*). Despite the presence of this naturalistic element, however, the room does not exhibit the *sukiya shoin* style to the extent seen in the Watanabe Residence. The larger proportions of the posts and frieze rails, for example, are appropriate to the administrative function of the Outer Zashiki as well as representative of contemporary taste. The difference between the *shoin* rooms of the Sasagawa and Watanabe houses may be related to subtle differences in family background and social status between the two families. Both houses, however, illustrate the fact that, by the late eighteenth and early nineteenth centuries, the *shoin* style had reached even the remote provinces of the country.

The Former Yakake Inn

The former Yakake Inn (the Ishii Residence) is one of the few remaining examples from the Edo period of a high-quality way station. It is particularly noteworthy because it retains not only a main inn (*honjin*) but a subsidiary inn (*waki-honjin*) as well. *Honjin* were officially designated for use by travelers of elevated status such as daimyo, government officials, or imperial messengers. *Waki-honjin* were put to use when no room was left in the *honjin* itself. Because of the high social status of the guests, *honjin* were supplied with elements of the *shoin* style. Perhaps the most detailed and certainly the most entertaining account in English of the atmosphere of one of these establishments is given by Oliver Statler in his *Japanese Inn*.

The Yakake Inn was a resting point for travelers on the San'yō Road, one of the eight main thoroughfares in premodern Japan. Running from Osaka southwest to Shimonoseki, the San'yō Road was the gateway to southern Honshu and Kyushu. It was one of the main roads used by the lords of the western provinces on their trips to and from Edo, trips necessitated by the "alternate attendance" (*sankin kōtai*) required by the shogunate.

The processions of a daimyo and his retinue were spectacles of pomp and splendor, employing hundreds of lancers, swordsmen, and porters, along with a group of bodyguards around the daimyo's palanquin. A doctor skilled in Chinese medical techniques was on hand as well to attempt to minimize the loss of life that not infrequently resulted from the rigors of these slow and arduous removals to and from Edo. Each clan had its own crest, its own lance style, and a variety of other identifying characteristics which would be prominently displayed as the procession advanced. Commoners would crouch down as the entourage wound past, and touch their heads to the ground. Porters carried poles on their shoulders from which were hung boxes containing weapons and armor, clothing, emergency food, equipment for baths, games, and curtains and folding seats for rest stops; in short, whatever might not be available at the inns at which they stopped. These inns were often reserved up to a year in advance in order that all would go with smoothness and decorum when the appointed day arrived.

The luxury and spaciousness of the Yakake Inn were necessitated by the importance of these elevated guests. Remarkably, over ten of its structures still remain, including the main house and the formal rooms. Since its proprietors, the Ishii family, were *sake* brewers as well as hostelers, the complex also includes storehouses for rice and finished *sake* as well as various buildings connected with the brewing process. These structures are arranged to either side of a central courtyard which runs from the entrance gate on the San'yō Road back through the Chūmon (Middle Gate) to the Ura-mon (Rear Gate; pl. 188). The main lodging structure fronts on the San'yō Road, with the formal rooms at the far right. These rooms can be directly entered via the Onari-mon (Processional Gate) and *genkan* directly in front of them or via the front and rear corridors running from the main house at the left of the formal reception rooms.

187. *Tokonoma* and staggered shelves of the Jōdan no Ma, former Yakake Inn.

The daimyo himself would take his ease in the Jōdan no Ma, the corner room at the rear of the formal section. Here he might sleep, or, as contemporary sources relate, read or be read to all night, preferring to sleep during the day to lessen the discomfort of his cramped palanquin as it lurched along on the shoulders of the two *kagokaki*. The Jōdan no Ma incorporates *shoin*-style elements as required by the high station of its occupant. These include a *jōdan* raised a step above the level of the anteroom, and a *tokonoma* and staggered shelves on the far wall (pl. 187). A *tsukeshoin* as well is set into the side with the veranda and overlaps the floor of the *tokonoma*. This arrangement resembles that of the Jōdan no Ma of the Sasagawa Residence, but evinces a more pronounced *sukiya* flavor, with thinner proportions and a naturalistically roughened lintel. The overall effect is one of dignified simplicity and restfulness, most appropriate for a lord's private chamber.

The former Yakake Inn and the Seisonkaku are the most recent buildings introduced in this survey. Although the exact age of the inn is unknown, it was probably constructed in the late Edo period, not long before the fall of the shogunate and the restoration of direct rule by the Meiji emperor in 1868. But though the feudal system in which the Yakake Inn was built passed away not long after the inn was completed, elements of the *shoin* style itself survived, and the delicate and balanced elements seen in the Jōdan no Ma of the inn remain the basis of the traditional-style architecture built in Japan today.

222

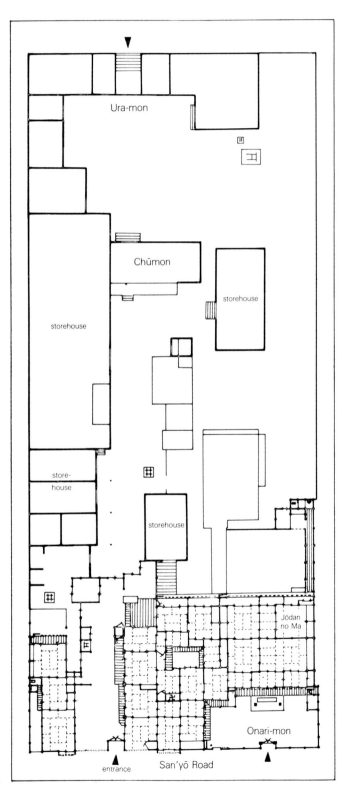

Ura-mon

Chūmon

storehouse

storehouse

store-
house

storehouse

Jōdan
no Ma

Onari-mon

entrance

San'yō Road

188. Plan of the former Yakake Inn.

NOTES TO THE TEXT

1   Translated by Donald Keene. In *Anthology of Japanese Literature: From the Earliest Era to the Mid-Nineteenth Century*, ed. Donald Keene (New York: Grove Press, 1955), p. 369.

2   Michael Cooper, S. J. *They Came to Japan* (Berkeley and Los Angeles: University of California Press, 1965), p. 118.

3   Robert T. Paine and Alexander C. Soper. *The Art and Architecture of Japan* (2nd ed., rev. New York: Penguin, 1975).

4   Hirai Kiyoshi. "The History of the Japanese House, Part 7." *Shin-kenchiku*, October 1977. In Japanese [平井聖「日本住宅の歴史 (7)」『新建築』昭和 52 年 10 月号].

5   Ōta Hirotarō. *The Shoin Style*. Tokyo: Tokyo Daigaku Shuppankai, 1966. In Japanese [太田博太郎『書院造』東京 東京大学出版会 昭和 41 年].

6   Cooper, *They Came to Japan*, p. 124.

7   Teiji Ito with Paul Novograd. "The Development of Shoin-style Architecture." In *Japan in the Muromachi Age*, ed. John W. Hall and Takeshi Toyoda. Berkeley: University of California Press, 1977.

8   Ōta Hirotarō, ed. *Traditional Japanese Architecture and Gardens*. Tokyo: Kokusai Bunka Shinkōkai, 1966.

9   Ōta, *Traditional Japanese Architecture and Gardens*, p. 44.

10   Arthur Drexler. *The Architecture of Japan*. New York: Museum of Modern Art, 1966.

11   Sei Shonagon. *The Pillow Book of Sei Shonagon*, trans. Ivan Morris (New York: Penguin, Classic Series, 1971), p. 262.

12   Sei Shonagon, *Pillow Book*, p. 66.

ADDRESSES OF SHOIN BUILDINGS

Daitsū-ji
Motohama-chō, Nagahama City
Shiga Prefecture

大通寺
滋賀県長浜市元浜町

Former Ichijō-in Imperial Apartments
Tōshōdai-ji
Nishinokyō-machi, Nara

唐招提寺旧一条院宸殿
奈良市西ノ京町

Former Yakake Inn
Yakake-chō, Oda-gun
Okayama Prefecture

旧矢掛本陣
岡山県小田郡矢掛町

Furui Residence
Ōkubo, Kumatori-chō, Sennan-gun
Osaka Prefecture

降井家住宅
大阪府泉南郡熊取町大久保

Ginkaku-ji (Jishō-ji)
Ginkakuji-machi, Sakyō-ku
Kyoto

銀閣寺（慈照寺）
京都市左京区銀閣寺町

Imanishi Residence
Imai-chō, Kashiwara City
Nara Prefecture

今西家住宅
奈良県橿原市今井町

Jikō-in Shoin
Koizumi-chō, Yamato-kōriyama City
Nara Prefecture

慈光院書院
奈良県大和郡山市小泉町

Kaitoku-kan, Kōchi Castle
Marunouchi, Kōchi City
Kōchi Prefecture

高知城懐徳館
高知県高知市丸ノ内

Kanchi-in Guest Hall, Kyōōgokoku-ji (Tō-ji)
Yanahara-chō, Ōmiyanishi-iru
Hachijō-dōri, Minami-ku, Kyoto

教王護国寺（東寺）観智院客殿
京都市南区八条通大宮西入ル柳原町

Kangaku-in Guest Hall, Onjō-ji
Onjōji-chō, Ōtsu City
Shiga Prefecture

園城寺勧学院客殿
滋賀県大津市園城寺町

Katsura Detached Palace
Katsura, Ukyō-ku
Kyoto

桂離宮
京都市右京区桂

Kinkaku-ji (Rokuon-ji)
Kinkakuji-chō, Kita-ku
Kyoto

金閣寺（鹿苑寺）
京都市北区金閣寺町

Kohō-an, Daitoku-ji
Daitokuji-chō, Murasakino
Kita-ku, Kyoto

大徳寺孤篷庵
京都市北区紫野大徳寺町

Kōjō-in Guest Hall, Onjō-ji
Onjōji-chō, Ōtsu City
Shiga Prefecture

園城寺光浄院客殿
滋賀県大津市園城寺町

Manshu-in Shoin
Takenouchi-chō, Ichijō-ji
Sakyō-ku, Kyoto
曼殊院書院
京都市左京区一乗寺竹ノ内町

Naka Residence
Gomon, Kumatori-chō, Sennan-gun
Osaka Prefecture
中家住宅
大阪府泉南郡熊取町五門

Ninomaru Palace, Nijō Castle
Horikawa Nishiiru, Nijō-dōri
Nakagyō-ku, Kyoto
二条城二の丸御殿
京都市中京区二条通堀川西入ル

Nishi Hongan-ji
Hanayamachi-kudaru, Horikawa-dōri
Shimogyō-ku, Kyoto
西本願寺
京都市下京区堀川通花屋町下ル

Reiun-in Shoin, Myōshin-ji
Hanazono Myōshinji-chō
Ukyō-ku, Kyoto
妙心寺霊雲院書院
京都市右京区花園妙心寺町

Rokuon-ji (see Kinkaku-ji)

Ryōgin-an Hōjō, Tōfuku-ji
15-chōme, Honchō
Higashiyama-ku, Kyoto
東福寺竜吟庵方丈
京都市東山区本町15丁目

Ryūkō-in Shoin, Daitoku-ji
Daitokuji-chō, Murasakino
Kita-ku, Kyoto
大徳寺竜光院書院
京都市北区紫野大徳寺町

Saikyō-ji Guest Hall
Sakamoto Honchō, Ōtsu City
Shiga Prefecture

西教寺客殿
滋賀県大津市坂本本町

Sambō-in, Daigo-ji
Daigo Higashiōji-chō
Fushimi-ku, Kyoto
醍醐寺三宝院
京都市伏見区醍醐東大路町

Sasagawa Residence
Ajikata-mura, Nishikanbara-gun
Niigata Prefecture
笹川家住宅
新潟県西蒲原郡味方村

Seisonkaku
Kenroku-chō, Kanazawa City
Ishikawa Prefecture
成巽閣
石川県金沢市兼六町

Shōgo-in Shoin
Shōgoin-nakamachi
Sakyō-ku, Kyoto
聖護院書院
京都市左京区聖護院中町

Shōjū Raigō-ji Guest Hall
Hieitsuji-machi, Shimosakamoto
Ōtsu City, Shiga Prefecture
聖衆来迎寺客殿
滋賀県大津市下坂本比叡辻町

Shugaku-in Detached Palace
Shugakuin Muromachi
Sakyō-ku, Kyoto
修学院離宮
京都市左京区修学院室町

Watanabe Residence
Shimoseki, Sekikawa-mura
Iwafune-gun, Niigata Prefecture
渡辺家住宅
新潟県岩船郡関川村大字下関

Yoshimizu Shrine Shoin
Yoshino-chō, Yoshino-gun
Nara Prefecture

吉水神社書院
奈良県吉野郡吉野町

Yoshimura Residence
Shimaizumi-chō, Habikino City
Osaka Prefecture

吉村家住宅

大阪府羽曳野市島泉町

Zuigan-ji Hondō
Matsushima-machi, Miyagi-gun
Miyagi Prefecture

瑞巌寺本堂
宮城県宮城郡松島町

LIST OF ILLUSTRATIONS IN JAPANESE

228

GLOSSARY

abbot's quarters. See *hōjō*.

battened ceiling. See *saobuchi tenjō*.

broad veranda. See *hiroen*.

buke-style architecture (武家造; *buke-zukuri*): a domestic style of architecture that begins to be seen in the houses of the warrior class in the Kamakura period. It had a stable, an area for samurai, and a characteristic gate. It was in general much like the *shinden* style, and scholars today consequently do not regard the *buke* style as a separate architectural type.

butsuma (仏間): a room for devotional purposes housing a Buddhist image.

ceiling frieze rail. See *nageshi*.

"Chinese" gable. See *karahafu*.

"Chinese" gate. See *karamon*.

"Chinese-style" architecture. See *karayō*.

chōdaigamae (帳台構): in the *shoin* style, decorative doors leading from the raised-floor section (*jōdan*) section into a secondary space. In some cases purely ornamental and nonopening. Originally the entrance doors opened into a sleeping and/or storage area. See plate 86.

chūmon (中門; "middle gate"): In a *shinden*-style dwelling, the gate bisecting the corridor (*chūmon-rō*) between a subsidiary living quarters (*tai-no-ya*) flanking the main *shinden* hall and a fountain pavilion. It was through this gate that ox carts, the favored conveyance of the nobility, entered the central courtyard. See plate 15.

chūmon-rō (中門廊; "middle gate corridor"): in the *shinden* style, the corridor between a subsidiary living quarters (*tai-no-ya*) flanking the main *shinden* hall and a fountain pavilion. Visitors often entered the main buildings via this corridor and it gradually abbreviated to the medieval *chūmon-rō*, a covered entrance arcade that projects from the corner of a building and serves as a formal entryway. One side is normally open and the other formed by a board wall. The medieval *chūmon-rō* is sometimes referred to as a *chūmon*. See plate 15.

daimedatami (台目畳; 代目畳; 大目畳): a three-quarter length *tatami* mat often found in teahouses or *sukiya shoin*. Possibly derived by subtracting the one-quarter-mat space occupied by the *furosakibyōbu* screen.

daimegamae (台目構): a construction found in many teahouses, consisting of a *daimedatami* and a center post (*nakabashira*), the latter of which is set into the corner of a sunken hearth (*ro*).

daimyō: a great lord. The name appears in the late Heian period in reference to great landholders. In the early Edo period a diamyo was the holder of a fief of over 10,000 *koku* of rice (1 *koku* equals approximately five bushels). The about 270 daimyo in this period were divided into *fudai* and *tozama* classes, the former being daimyo who were allied with the Tokugawa before Ieyasu grasped absolute power at the battle of Sekigahara, and the latter those who submitted only afterward.

decorative molding. See *kamachi*.

doma (土間): in *minka*, an unfloored, usually earthen space used as a work area. Also called a *niwa*. See plate 178.

Edo period (1615–1867): the period during which the Tokugawa shogunate held power. Tokugawa Ieyasu (1542–1616) located his headquarters in Edo (modern Tokyo). Soon after coming to power, the shogunate forbade Christian worship and most contact with foreign countries. This "closed country" policy remained in force for over two centuries. The period ended when the Tokugawa were overthrown and the Meiji emperor restored to power fifteen years after the arrival of Commodore Perry. The merchant class became economically powerful in the Edo period and generated its own characteristic culture.

The *shoin* style reached its most lavish stage early in the period. Concurrently elements of teahouse architecture were incorporated into the *shoin* scheme to produce the *sukiya shoin*. This style gradually diffused into the homes of the commoners.

frieze rails. See *nageshi*.

fusuma (襖): interior sliding screens covered with heavy paper on both sides and usually decorated with paintings (*fusuma-e*) or calligraphy. They function as room partitions. *Fusuma* is an abbreviation of *fusuma-shōji*.

gedan (下段): the lower floor area in front of the raised floor (*jōdan*) in a formal *shoin* room or in front of the middle-level (*chūdan*) floor space. Used by those of lower rank. See plate 2, foreground.

genkan (玄関): entrance hall, used as the formal entrance area for visitors of high rank. One or more steps at the end abutting on the main building provide for the transition from ground to floor level. In Zen abbot's quarters (*hōjō*) the *genkan* is a large space, usually at least one bay wide by two bays deep, that projects from the main structure (pls. 80–81). In the Edo period an entry hall with a built-in plank floor section (*shikidai*) was incorporated into homes of the upper classes, and its use was regulated by sumptuary laws.

goza no ma (御座の間): in a *shoin* mansion, the master's private room or suite. Also *gyoza no ma*.

Heian period (782–1184): This period began with the removal of the national capital to Heian-kyō, or modern Kyoto, and ended nearly four centuries later with the establishment of the military regime of Minamoto no Yoritomo (1147–99) in Kamakura. Government was centered in the court, with, for much of the period, power held in theory by the emperor and in practice by regents of the Fujiwara family. Although Chinese influence was still marked during the first century of the Heian period, it weakened with the demise of the T'ang dynasty toward the end of the ninth century, and a native culture of great elegance and sophistication developed. The Heian capital was designed on a grid plan after the T'ang capital of Ch'ang-an. The nobility lived in mansions built in the *shinden* style.

hiradana (平棚; "flat shelf"): a single plank, used as a shelf in an alcove (see plate 29) or as a writing surface (see plate 170).

hirashoin (平書院; "flat *shoin*"): an abbreviated *tsukeshoin* that dispenses with the alcove and the writing desk but retains the *shōji*, flush against the wall. See plate 168.

hiroen (広縁; "broad veranda"): a wide veranda beyond the *shōji* screens but under the eaves. Often bounded by an outer veranda (*ochien*) one step lower. See plate 57.

hiroma (広間): refers either to the most formal room of late Momoyama or early Edo *shoin*, or to the entire building housing that room. Literally meaning "large space," the name as applied to an entire structure is thought to have originated with the Hiroma of Hideyoshi's Juraku-dai castle-palace, which was an enlarged version of the earlier *shuden* style. Also called *ōhiroma*.

hōjō (方丈): the abbot's quarters of a Zen monastery. It is usually comprised of two rows of three rooms each, with the center room of the back row containing an altar and the corner room next to it being used as the abbot's private study.

hongawara roofing (本瓦葺; *hongawara-buki*): a style of tile roofing using vertical rows of gently curved tiles (*hiragawara*), concave side up, with half-cylindrical tiles (*marugawara*), concave side down, over the interstices between the rows of *hiragawara*. The *marugawara* at the roof edges have circular facings with decorative motifs. See plate 115.

ichi no ma (一の間; "first room"): one of the

names for the most elegant space in a structure. It is usually reserved for formal meetings. Includes all or some of the *shoin* accoutrements.

"Japanese-style" architecture. See *wayō*.

jōdan (上段): the area in a formal *shoin* that is raised one step. The *tokonoma*, staggered shelves, *tsukeshoin*, and *chōdaigamae* are located around its periphery. Used by the ranking personage at audiences in order to underscore his superior station. See plate 84.

Jōdo-shū (Pure Land sect): a Buddhist sect teaching that one need only recite the name of the Amida (Amitābha) Buddha, "Lord of Infinite Light," to be reborn in the Pure Land, Amida's "Western Paradise." A simpler teaching than the Tendai and Shingon creeds, it was popularized by Hōnen (1133–1212) and thereafter became a major sect, particularly among warriors and commoners. Shinran (1175–1262), a disciple of Hōnen, went on to found Jōdo Shinshū (True Pure Land sect), also known as Shinshū or Ikkō-shū.

jōjōdan (上々段): an auxiliary area one step above the main raised-floor space (*jōdan*), usually for private use. See plate 100.

kamachi (框): a decorative molding, often lacquered, fit on the front of raised *tokonoma* and shelf alcove floors and the *jōdan* step. See plates 2–3.

Kamakura period (1185–1332): In the late Heian period, two powerful warrior families vied for power, with the Minamoto (Genji) clan defeating the Taira (Heike) in 1185. Minamoto no Yoritomo (1147–99) thereupon established his government in Kamakura and held de facto rule as *seii-tai-shōgun* ("Barbarian-quelling Generalissimo"). The period ended with the overthrow of the last Kamakura shogun and his regent of the Hōjō family by forces of Emperor Godaigo (1288–1339).

During the Kamakura period the Zen Buddhist creed was brought into the country from Sung China and found favor first with the military. The Zen monks exerted a strong influence on Japanese culture, introducing, for example, Zen temple architecture from China. This consequently became known as *karayō* or "Chinese-style" architecture, and it played a major role in the development of the *shoin* style. It was in this period as well that some residences came to use square rather than round posts, sliding screens, *tatami* mats, ceilings, and *mairado* exterior screens, all these being *shoin*-style characteristics.

karahafu (唐破風): Literally "Chinese gable," but thought to have originated in Japan, the *karahafu* is a bow-shaped gable used on elegant buildings and gates. See plate 90.

karamon (唐門): Literally "Chinese gate," but its debt to Chinese sources is questionable. Its "Chinese" gables (*karahafu*) are located on both ends in the case of a *hira-karamon* (平唐門) and on the front and back in that of a *mukai-karamon* (向唐門). *Karamon* are often found in front of *monzeki* temples and abbot's quarters. See plate 104.

karayō (唐様; "Chinese style"): in architecture, the name given to the temple style of Sung China when it was introduced into Japan together with the Zen creed in the late twelfth century. Contrasts with the *wayō* or "Japanese-style" temple architecture developed from modes introduced from the continent about the time of the T'ang dynasty. The main characteristics of *karayō* architecture include ornate bracketing with carved nosing over not only the columns but the intercolumnar spaces as well, fan raftering, paneled Chinese-style doors, and ogee-arched windows. Also called the *zenshū-yō* (禅宗様) or Zen style.

kegomiita (蹴込み板): the narrow, recessed wall space between the *tatami* mats and the floorboard of a *tokonoma*, shelf alcove, or *tsukeshoin*. See plates 2–3.

kokabe (小壁; "small wall"): the narrow wall space between the mid-wall and ceiling circumferential frieze rails. See plates 2–3.

kuri (庫裏; 庫裡): the kitchens of a Zen temple. Often also includes a living space for monks and a guest area.

kurumayose (車寄; "carriage approach"): an entrance porch, often for alighting from a cart or palanquin. Can have simply a door and curved "Chinese" gable, or be an entire enclosed space. One characteristic of the *shinden* or *shuden* styles, as well as some early *shoin* structures. See plate 67.

mairado (舞良戸): a sliding wooden door faced with thin, closely spaced wooden strips. Used on the exterior of early *shoin* structures. Frequently appears in a combination of two *mairado* and one *shōji* per bay. See plate 67.

Meiji period (1868–1912): corresponds to the reign of the Meiji Emperor (b. 1852) who ascended the throne on the overthrow of the Tokugawa shogunate. The monarchy was restored to a position of actual power and Japan began the process of Westernization. Western forms of architecture began to be used in place of, or together with, traditional styles.

menkawa post (面皮柱; *menkawa-bashira*): a post with planed sides but unplaned corners. On these corners the bark is either retained or peeled off to show the rough texture of the original log. Often used in *sukiya shoin* structures, the *menkawa* post reflects the emphasis on simplicity and nature implicit in tea taste. The *menkawa* technique is also occasionally used on frieze rails and ceiling battens. See plate 164.

minka (民家): premodern residences of the common people, as opposed to those of the civil and military aristocracy and the clergy. *Minka* can be in general divided into two broad classes, the farmhouse (*nōka*), such as the Yoshimura Residence (pl. 176), and the urban house (*machiya*), exemplified by the Imanishi Residence (pl. 172).

Momoyama period (1568–1614): During the short Momoyama period Japan was reunified by three successive generals—

Oda Nobunaga (1534–82), Toyotomi Hideyoshi (1536–98), and Tokugawa Ieyasu (1542–1616), ending a century of civil war. It was a period of artistic rebirth and decorative magnificence, with massive gold and polychrome screen painting reaching perfection. Conversely, the tea ceremony attained at this time its greatest rusticity and simplicity. This was the great period of castle building and the flowering of the *shoin* style.

monzeki (門跡): a temple in which resides a member of the royal family or high nobility who has taken Buddhist orders. The term can also refer to that person. A *miya-monzeki* (宮門跡) houses a member of the royal family, a *sekke-monzeki* (摂家門跡) a member of one of the five "regency houses" (*sekke*), and a *seika-monzeki* (清花門跡) a member of one of the seven noble families ranked just below the five regency houses. A *jun-monzeki* (准門跡) or *waki-monzeki* (脇門跡) is a religious establishment under the jurisdiction of a *monzeki* temple. These ranks were systematized in the Edo period and remain in unofficial use today.

munafuda (棟札; ridgepole certificate): a record of the carpenter, sponsor, date, and other pertinent details about a building project that is written on a wooden tag and fastened to the roof ridgepole or, occasionally, written directly on the ridgepole during building construction or renovation.

Muromachi period (1333–1567): the era of the Ashikaga shogunate. The period from 1336 to 1392 is also referred to as the era of the Northern and Southern courts (Nambokuchō), in which two rival courts vied for ascendency. Ruling from Kyoto, the Ashikaga shoguns were strongly influenced by the aestheticism of the court and the philosophy of Zen. The tea ceremony, Nō drama, and Chinese-style ink painting reached maturity during this era. During the later Muromachi period the country descended into anarchy, this era being known as the Age of the Country at War (*sengoku jidai*; 1467–1568).

In architecture, this was the period that the *tokonoma* (*oshiita*), built-in shelves, and *jōdan* came into common use, together with the *tsukeshoin* alcove which developed somewhat earlier. The oldest extant *shoin* structure, the Tōgu-dō of Shogun Ashikaga Yoshimasa (1435–90), dates from this period.

nageshi (長押; circumferential frieze rail): Although originally a tie-beam, in the *shoin* style the *nageshi*, or circumferential frieze rail, has no structural function and is instead an ornamental member indicating a formal *shoin*-style room. Mid-wall frieze rails (内法長押; *uchinori nageshi*) are located just above the *fusuma* screens, and ceiling frieze rails (天井長押; *tenjō nageshi*) encircle the room just beneath the ceiling. See plates 2–3.

nando (納戸): a room for storage and/or sleeping. Often with three fixed walls and *chōdaigamae* (*nandogamae*) doors. Rooms called *nurigome* (塗籠) or *chōdai* (帳代) often have the same function.

ni no ma (二の間; "second room"): one of the names for the anteroom of the most formal *shoin* space. Called in some buildings the *tsugi no ma* (次の間; "next room").

Nō: a dramatic form perfected in the fifteenth century and adopted as the official entertainment of the warrior class. Slow, stylized, and symbolic, the Nō was profoundly influenced by the aesthetics of Zen. It is acted and danced by one main character, who wears gorgeously embroidered robes and a mask. He is supported by a small number of subsidiary actors, musicians, and chorus.

ochien (落縁; outer veranda): a veranda located beyond and a step below the main floor area or the broad veranda (*hiroen*). See plate 57.

ōhiroma. See *hiroma*.

oshiita (押板): an early *tokonoma* alcove characterized by shallow depth and pronounced width, high and thick lintel, and a thick floorboard (*oshiita*) made of a single plank with no decorative molding (*kamachi*) and separated from the *tatami* mats by a narrow recessed wall space (*kegomiita*).

outer veranda. See *ochien*.

Pure Land sect. See Jōdo-shū.

ramma. *See* transom.

reticulated shutters. See *shitomido*.

ridgepole certificate. See *munafuda*.

sangawara roofing (桟瓦葺; *sangawara-buki*): pantile roofing. A style of tile roofing invented in the early Edo period that uses tiles gently S-shaped in cross section with the concave side of one overlapped by the convex side of the next. See plate 160.

sankin kōtai (参勤交代): a shogunal law requiring daimyo to spend a period of time at set intervals in Edo, away from their home fiefs. Put into effect to discourage rebellion.

san no ma (三の間; "third room"): adjoins the *ni no ma* ("second room").

saobuchi tenjō (竿縁天井; battened ceiling): a ceiling of wooden planks and battens (*saobuchi*) running the ceiling length at right angles to the planks. The battens are made of cedar, cypress, or even bamboo, and are squared off in formal *shoin* but often left partially unfinished in *sukiya shoin* structures. Spaced at intervals of thirty to forty centimeters, they sometimes provide support for ceiling planks and some times are purely decorative. See plate 133.

seirō-dana (城楼棚; 清楼棚): one of the most frequently used types of shelves, having a three-part structure with the central shelf raised above the flanking ones. See plate 88.

shikidai (式台): in the Momoyama and early Edo periods, a formal room (*shikidai no ma*) for greeting or seeing off guests. Later, the plank floor in front of the entrance hall (*genkan*) takes over this function, that floor becoming known as the *shikidai*.

shinden (宸殿; "imperial apartments"): a structure presented to a temple from an imperial palace.

235

shinden (寝殿; "sleeping hall"): the main building in a *shinden*-style residential complex.

shinden style (寝殿造; *shinden-zukuri*): the residential style of the upper classes in the Heian and Kamakura periods. Consists of a central hall (*shinden*) with a central space (*moya*) and subsidiary spaces (*hisashi*) radiating therefrom, round columns, wooden floors, and reticulated shutters (*shitomido*). Ideally the *shinden* complex was bilaterally symmetrical and faced south, with the central hall connected to flanking halls (*tai-no-ya*) by means of corridors (*chūmon-rō*). These corridors then extended south from the *tai-no-ya* to small kiosklike pavilions which bordered on a garden and pond. See plate 15.

Shingon sect (True Word sect): an outgrowth of Tantric Buddhism. Its headquarters are located on Mount Kōya in Wakayama Prefecture. Shingon was formulated by Kūkai (posthumously Kōbō Daishi; 774–835) and is characterized by spectacular ritual and mysticism.

shitomido (蔀戸; reticulated shutters): a reticulated, shutterlike exterior door. Can be opened by swinging up the top half and fastening it to the eaves with a long metal hanger and removing the bottom half from between the columns. Used in *shinden* and some early *shoin* buildings as well as in temples. See plate 56.

shoin (書院): an early term for what is now known as the *tsukeshoin* or the study room in which this desk was located. Also a whole building or complex in the *shoin* style.

shoin style (書院造; *shoin-zukuri*): a style of residential architecture first appearing in the Muromachi period and used in general in the mansions of the military, temple guest halls, and Zen Buddhist abbot's quarters in the Momoyama and Edo periods. It is characterized by a complex of buildings, often separated by function, the main room or rooms of which includes a *tokonoma*, staggered shelves, writing alcove (*tsukeshoin*), and decorative doors (*chōdai-gamae*), or some combination thereof, often on a raised-floor area (*jōdan*), together with *tatami*-mat floors, sliding screens, verandas, square posts, ceilings, and, in the Edo period, an entryway (*genkan*).

shōji (障子): exterior sliding screens constructed of a single layer of opaque paper pasted to one side of a wooden latticed frame. Contracted form of *akarishōji* (明り障子). See plate 52.

shuden (主殿; "principal hall"): the central building in a *shuden*-style complex. It first appears in warrior mansions of the Kamakura period. In the fifteenth century it becomes the living area of the residential complex, with the earlier *shinden* hall retained for traditional formal ceremonies.

shuden style (主殿造; *shuden-zukuri*): a style of architecture classed variously as the precursor of the *shoin* style or as an early version of that style. The main hall (*shuden*) retains some of the earlier *shinden*-style elements, such as the *chūmon-rō* corridor and reticulated shutters (*shitomido*), but also includes many of the *shoin*-style characteristics like the *shikidai*, raised-floor area (*jōdan*), square posts, *tatami* flooring, *fusuma* interior partitions, *shōji* sliding screens, wooden sliding screens (*mairado*), the *tokonoma* (*oshiita*) shelves, writing alcove (*tsukeshoin*), and decorative doors (*chōdai-gamae*). The guest halls of the Kangaku-in and Kōjō-in subtemples of Onjō-ji best exemplify the style. In the Momoyama period the *shuden* is expanded, becoming known as the *hiroma*.

sliding screens. See *fusuma*; *shōji*.

sodekabe (袖壁): in a *chōdaigamae*, the two fixed outer doors (pl. 7). In a tearoom, a wall, open at the bottom, that reaches from the side of the room to the center post, and often has shelves (*tsuridana*) attached to the back (pl. 161).

sukiya (数寄屋): a teahouse, or a building in the *sukiya shoin* style.

sukiya shoin style (数寄屋書院造; *sukiya shoin-zukuri*): a blend of the formal *shoin* style and teahouse elements. Characterized in general by a free and innovative arrangement of the main design elements, posts with unplaned corners, absence of a raised-floor area (*jōdan*) and decorative doors (*chōdaigamae*), often colored walls and a relaxed and informal mood. Frequently abbreviated "*sukiya* style."

tatami (畳): straw rectangular mats of approximately one meter by two meters in size, though dimensions vary according to geographical locale. Laid side by side to constitute flooring. The size of a room is usually represented by the number of *tatami* mats it contains.

Tendai sect: an eclectic sect of Buddhism based on the Lotus Sutra. Introduced into Japan by Saichō (posthumously Dengyō Daishi; 767–822), it gradually became imbued with the Esoteric teachings of the Shingon sect. Its monks formed armies and periodically descended on the capital from their central monastery, atop Mount Hiei.

tenjō nageshi. See *nageshi*.

tokobashira (床柱; "*tokonoma* post"): the post located at the side of the *tokonoma* opposite the veranda, and thus near the center of the main wall. It is often of extremely fine wood and craftsmanship as it is a focal point of a room's interior design. In the *sukiya shoin* it is usually left partially or completely unplaned for natural effect. See plates 137–38.

tokonoma (床間): in the Kamakura and Muromachi periods, a raised floor, platform, or bench. In the Momoyama period and after, an alcove with a raised floorboard and lowered lintel, usually used for the display of a piece of art.

tokonoma post. See *tokobashira*.

transom (欄間; *ramma*): refers to a high, open-work partition, usually of wood or bamboo, between two spaces. Built just above head level, it often has runners beneath it for sliding screens. Designed in a multitude of styles, these transoms serve as a major element of interior design. See plates 100, 135.

tsugi no ma. See *ni no ma*.

tsukeshoin (付書院): a low surface for reading or writing located in an alcove which projects into a veranda and is fitted with *shōji*. Originally known as a *shoin, dashifuzukue*, etc.

uchinori nageshi. See *nageshi*.

wayō (和様; "Japanese style"): in temple architecture, used in contrast to the later *karayō*, or "Chinese style," imported from the continent. The term *wayō* was coined to distinguish this, the earlier mode of temple building, from the *karayō*, and is itself actually of Chinese origin as well, though from the Six Dynasties and T'ang periods. The style was, however, further developed in Japan. It is characterized by, among other elements, brackets used only above the columns and not the intercolumnar spans, parallel rafters instead of radial ones, rectangular windows instead of ogee-arched designs, and solid wooden doors rather than paneled "Chinese-style" types (*sankarado*).

Zen: a Buddhist teaching introduced from Sung China by two monks, Dōgen (1200–53) and Eisai (1141–1215). It stresses enlightenment by one's own efforts, through seated meditation (*zazen*) and/or contemplation of paradoxical questions (*kōan*). Zen monks played a vital role as advisors to the government in not only religious matters but also trade with China and cultural affairs.

Zen-style architecture. See *karayō*.

BIBLIOGRAPHY

JAPANESE SOURCES
(selected and annotated by the author)

文化庁監修『重要文化財』第16巻（建造物 V）東京 毎日新聞社 昭和50年 [Agency for Cultural Affairs of the Japanese Government. *Important Cultural Properties*, vol. 16. (Architecture V). Tokyo: Mainichi Shimbunsha, 1975].
The set in which this volume appears lists all the art and architecture designated Important Cultural Properties by the Japanese government. Includes a photograph and short explanation for each entry, along with a plan in the case of architecture. Volume 16 includes castles, *shoin*, and teahouses.

藤岡通夫『城と書院』（原色日本の美術 12）東京 小学館 昭和46年 [Fujioka, Michio. *Castles and Shoin*. Japanese Art in Color, vol. 12. Tokyo: Shōgakkan, 1971].
Covers extant representative castles and *shoin* buildings, with photographs, figures, and explanations for the general reader.

—— 恒成一訓共著『書院』全2巻 東京 創元社 昭和44年 [——, and Tsunenari, Kazukuni. *Shoin*. 2 vols. Tokyo: Sōgensha, 1969].
Presents *shoin* buildings designated Important Cultural Properties by the Japanese government. With photographs, plans, and commentaries.

藤原義一『書院造の研究』高桐書院 昭和21年 [Fujiwara, Giichi. *Studies on the Shoin Style*. Tokyo: Kōtō Shoin. 1946].
A collection of basic research on the *shoin* style, including comparisons of plans and details of extant structures and an investigation of the origins of the *tokonoma* and other elements of the style.

平井 聖『日本住宅の歴史』東京 日本放送出版協会 昭和49年 [Hirai, Kiyoshi. *The History of Japanese Domestic Architecture*. Tokyo: Nihon Hōsō Shuppan Kyōkai, 1974].

——『日本の近世住宅』東京 鹿島研究所出版会 昭和43年 [——. *Japanese Domestic Architecture of the Early Modern Period*. Tokyo: Kajima Kenkyūjo Shuppankai, 1968].
Uses research into shogunal palaces such as that of Edo Castle and records of shogunal visits to clarify the functions of the warrior residence in the early modern era. Discusses the development of the *shoin* plan and of the style in general.

堀口捨己『茶室』（日本の美術 83）東京 至文堂 昭和48年 [Horiguchi, Sutemi. *Teahouses*. Arts of Japan, vol. 83. Tokyo: Shibundō, 1973].
An introduction to teahouse architecture, this work is based primarily on photographs and shows the relationship between the teahouse and the *shoin* style.

——『利休の茶室』東京 鹿島研究所出版会 昭和43年 [——. *The Teahouses of Sen no Rikyū*. Tokyo: Kajima Kenkyūjo Shuppankai, 1968].
Teahouses are the basis of the *sukiya shoin* style, and Horiguchi's works on them are

especially valuable. Chapter 8 of this book, detailing the development of the *sukiya shoin* style, is particularly noteworthy.

川上　貢『日本中世住宅史研究』東京 墨水書房　昭 42 年　[Kawakami, Mitsugu. *Studies on Japanese Domestic Architecture of the Medieval Period*. Tokyo: Bokusui Shobō, 1967].
Reconstructs residences of the medieval aristocracy by means of contemporary documents, and investigates the manner in which homes were used, the way public and private uses differed, and the change from the *shinden* to the *shoin* style.

森　蘊『桂離宮』東京 毎日新聞社　昭和 45 年　[Mori, Osamu. *Katsura Detached Palace*. Tokyo: Mainichi Shimbunsha, 1970].

———『修学院離宮』東京 毎日新聞社　昭和 45 年　[———. *Shugaku-in Detached Palace*. Tokyo: Mainichi Shimbunsha, 1970].

———『桂離宮』（日本の美術 79）東京 至文堂　昭和 47 年　[———. *Katsura Detached Palace*. Arts of Japan, vol. 79. Tokyo: Shibundō, 1972].

———『修学院離宮』（日本の美術 112）東京 至文堂　昭和 50 年　[———. *Shugaku-in Detached Palace*. Arts of Japan, vol. 112. Tokyo: Shibundō, 1975].
The above four works are related to two imperial villas which cannot be visited without special permission. They are based primarily on photographs, with appended commentary.

野地脩左『中世住宅史研究』東京 日本学術振興会　昭和 30 年　[Noji, Shūsa. *Studies on the History of Medieval Domestic Architecture*. Tokyo: Nihon Gakujutsu Shinkōkai, 1955].
Research on the Tōgu-dō based on documents from the late Muromachi period, investigation of the development and architectural implications of the *tokonoma*, and a discussion of the names for rooms used in the medieval period. Other scholars, however, hold views that differ from those presented here.

岡田　譲編『床の間と床飾り』（日本の美術 152）東京 至文堂　昭和 54 年　[Okada, Yuzuru, ed. *Tokonoma and Tokonoma Decoration*. Arts of Japan, vol. 152. Tokyo: Shibundō, 1979].
Discusses the development and use of the *tokonoma*, the central element of the *shoin* main room, and shows how the Japanese-style house of today developed from the *shoin* style in response to changing life styles.

太田博太郎『図説日本住宅史』東京 彰国社　昭和 23 年　[Ōta, Hirotarō. *Illustrated History of Japanese Domestic Architecture*. Tokyo: Shōkokusha, 1948].
A useful overview of the development of the Japanese house from prehistoric times to the present.

———『日本住宅史』（建築学大系 1）彰国社　昭和 31 年　[———. *The History of Japanese Domestic Architecture*. Outline of Architectural History, vol. 1. Tokyo: Shōkokusha, 1956].

———『書院造』東京 東京大学出版会　昭和 41 年　[———. *The Shoin Style*. Tokyo: Tokyo Daigaku Shuppankai, 1966].
A work discussing the development of the *shoin* style on the basis of recent research reports. At present the most easily understood work on the *shoin* style. The bibliography is one of the most complete as well.

———『床の間』東京 岩波書店　昭和 53 年　[———. *Tokonoma*. Tokyo: Iwanami Shoten, 1978].
Discusses the development and use of the *tokonoma*, the central element of the *shoin* main

room, and shows how the Japanese-style house of today developed from the *shoin* style in response to changing life styles.

—— 監修・川上 貢著『日本建築史基礎資料集成』第16巻（書院 I）東京 中央公論美術出版 昭和46年 [——, series ed. *Compilation of Basic Materials on Japanese Architectural History*. Vol. 16 (Shoin I), by Kawakami Mitsugu. Tokyo: Chūō Kōron Bijutsu Shuppan, 1971].

—— 監修・平井 聖著『日本建築史基礎資料集成』第17巻（書院 II）東京 中央公論美術出版 昭和49年 [——, series ed. *Compilation of Basic Materials on Japanese Architectural History*. Vol. 17 (Shoin II), by Hirai Kiyoshi. Tokyo: Chūō Kōron Bijutsu Shuppan, 1974].

In the two entries above, volume 16 covers *shoin* dating to the early Edo period, and volume 17 those thereafter. Valuable reference works for specialists, they include many plans and photographs as well as scholarly explanations.

FURTHER READING
(selected and annotated by the translator)

Asano, Kiichi (photographs), and Takakura, Gisel (commentary). *Japanese Gardens Revisited*. Adapted by Frank Davies and Hirokuni Kobatake. Vermont and Tokyo: Tuttle, 1973. Short commentaries on Japanese gardens and a large number of color photographs.

Blaser, Werner. *Japanese Temples and Tea Houses*. New York: Dodge, 1956. A Western architect's introduction to seeing Japanese architectural space, with emphasis on Katsura. Artistically conceived photographs.

Conder, Josiah. *Landscape Gardening in Japan*. 1893. Reprint. New York: Dover, 1964. A pioneer work of historic interest by the first Instructor of Architecture at the Imperial University.

Cooper, Michael. *They Came to Japan*. Berkeley and Los Angeles: University of California Press, 1965. Accounts of Japan by foreigners during the "Christian century" preceding the closing of the country in the early Edo period. Valuable here for its firsthand descriptions of contemporary architecture.

Doi, Tsuguyoshi. *Momoyama Decorative Painting*. Translated and adapted by Edna B. Crawford. Heibonsha Survey of Japanese Art, vol. 14. New York and Tokyo: Weatherhill and Heibonsha, 1977. An overview of the large-scale mural painting of the kind used in *shoin* buildings. Particularly relevant here is the chapter on these paintings and castles.

Drexler, Arthur. *The Architecture of Japan*. New York: Museum of Modern Art, 1966. A general and very readable discussion of Japanese architecture, concentrating on several representative structures.

Engel, Heinrich. *The Japanese House: A Tradition for Contemporary Architecture*. Vermont and Tokyo: Tuttle, 1964. A very detailed treatment of the Japanese house. Profusely illustrated with line drawings and photographs of every element of the Japanese residence.

Fukuda, Kazuhiko. *Japanese Stone Gardens: How to Make and Enjoy Them.* Vermont and Tokyo: Tuttle, 1970.
> An introduction to one type of Japanese garden. Liberal use of old illustrations and an interesting section on how stone gardens are constructed.

Futagawa, Yukio (photographs), and Itō, Teiji (text). *The Roots of Japanese Architecture.* Translated by Paul Konya. New York: Harper and Row, 1963.
> A fine book of photographs, those of *sukiya* and *minka* architecture being of value here.

Grilli, Elise. *The Art of the Japanese Garden.* New York and Tokyo: Weatherhill, 1970.
> Discussion of representative screen paintings. Beautifully illustrated.

Hayashiya, Tatsusaburo; Nakamura, Masao; and Hayashiya, Seizo. *Japanese Arts and the Tea Ceremony.* Translated and adapted by Joseph P. Macadam. Heibonsha Survey of Japanese Art, vol. 15. New York and Tokyo: Weatherhill and Heibonsha, 1974.
> An introduction to the development of the tea ceremony and teahouse architecture.

Hirai, Kiyoshi. *Feudal Architecture of Japan.* Translated and adapted by Hiroaki Sato and Jeannine Ciliotta. Heibonsha Survey of Japanese Art, vol. 13. New York and Tokyo: Weatherhill and Heibonsha, 1973.
> A detailed treatment of the *shoin* style, with a long section on castle architecture as well. Particularly strong on design developments.

―――. "The History of the Japanese House, Part 7." *Shinkenchiku,* October 1977. In Japanese [―――「日本住宅の歴史 (7)」『新建築』昭和 52 年 10 月号].
> New theories about the maturation process of the *shoin* style.

Ishimoto, Yasuhiro. *Katsura: Tradition and Creation in Japanese Architecture.* Texts by Walter Gropius and Kenzo Tange. Translated by Charles Terry. New Haven: Yale University Press, 1960.
> Valuable for its fine photographs of *sukiya* detail at Katsura. Includes a subjective essay on general Japanese architecture by Gropius and a longer piece on Katsura by Tange.

Ito, Teiji. *The Elegant Japanese House: Traditional Sukiya Architecture.* New York and Tokyo: Walker and Weatherhill, 1969.
> A lyric approach to old and new *sukiya* dwellings. Superb plates.

―――. *The Japanese Garden: An Approach to Nature.* Photographs by Takeji Iwamiya. Translated by Donald Richie. New Haven and London: Yale University Press, 1972.
> A short, chronological introduction covering the major garden types. Fine color and black-and-white plates.

―――. *Traditional Domestic Architecture of Japan.* Translated and adapted by Richard L. Gage. Heibonsha Survey of Japanese Art, vol. 21. New York and Tokyo: Weatherhill and Heibonsha, 1972.
> A survey of the *minka* and its structural and regional variations.

―――. *Space and Illusion in the Japanese Garden.* Photographs by Sosei Kuzunishi. Translated and adapted by Ralph Friedrich and Masajiro Shimamura. New York and Tokyo: Weatherhill and Tankosha, 1973.
> Focuses on the open garden which incorporates outlying scenery (or *shakkei*, "borrowed scenery") and the enclosed courtyard garden. Effective photography.

―――, with Paul Novograd. "The Development of Shoin-style Architecture." In *Japan in*

the Muromachi Age, edited by John W. Hall and Takeshi Toyoda. Berkeley: University of California Press, 1977.
A clear and concise explanation of the transition from the *shinden* to the *shoin* style and the accompanying shifts in social customs.

Kidder, Edward. *Japanese Temples*. Tokyo: Bijutsu Shuppansha, 1966.
Covers the sculpture, painting, gardens, and architecture of a select number of Japanese temples, the sections on Kinkaku-ji, Ginkaku-ji, and Daitoku-ji being directly relevant to the study of *shoin*.

Kirby, John B. *From Castle to Teahouse: Japanese Architecture of the Momoyama Period*. Vermont and Tokyo: Tuttle, 1962.
A worthwhile introduction to the architecture of the Momoyama and early Edo periods.

Kitao, Harumichi. *Shoin Architecture in Detailed Illustrations*. Tokyo: Shōkokusha, 1956.
A collection of line drawings and photographs of *shoin* structures and design details. Good handbook for *shoin* architectural terminology.

Kuck, Loraine. *The World of the Japanese Garden*. Photography by Takeji Iwamiya. New York and Tokyo: Walker and Weatherhill, 1968.
An ambitious work reaching from early Chinese garden examples to the modern period. Fine color plates by a master of garden photography.

Morse, Edward. *Japanese Homes and Their Surroundings*. 1896. Reprint. Vermont and Tokyo: Tuttle, 1972.
An early study of Japanese domestic architecture. Rich in detail and well illustrated with drawings by the author.

Naitō, Akira. *Katsura: A Princely Retreat*. Photography by Takeshi Nishikawa. Translated by Charles S. Terry. Tokyo and New York: Kodansha International, 1977.
The most luxurious of the books on Katsura in English, with superb color plates, very good plans and elevations, and an up-to-date commentary.

Okawa, Naomi. *Edo Architecture: Katsura and Nikko*. Photography by Chuji Hirayama. Translated and adapted by Alan Woodhull and Akito Miyamoto. Heibonsha Survey of Japanese Art, vol. 20. New York and Tokyo: Weatherhill and Heibonsha, 1975.
An in-depth treatment of two very different approaches to Japanese architecture in the Edo period, the Katsura section being particularly relevant to *shoin* studies. Includes a good section on *wayō* and *karayō* styles.

Ota, Hirotaro, ed. *Traditional Japanese Architecture and Gardens*. Tokyo: Kokusai Bunka Shin-kōkai, 1966 (condensed ed., 1972).
A very good overall introduction to Japanese architecture and gardens by some of the leading Japanese scholars in the field.

————. *Introduction to Japanese Architectural History*. Tokyo: Shōkokusha, 1969. In Japanese [太田博太郎『日本建築史序説』東京 彰国社 昭和44年].
A chronological overview of Japanese architecture from prehistory to the introduction of Western styles. The last third of the work is an exhaustive bibliography.

Paine, Robert T., and Soper, Alexander C. *The Art and Architecture of Japan*. 2nd ed., rev. New York: Penguin, 1975.

A basic introductory text to Japanese art and architecture. The sections on the *shoin* style have been up-dated by Bunji Kobayashi, who also added a helpful summary of pertinent articles in the *Japan Architect*, the English version of *Shinkenchiku*, a monthly magazine published by Shinkenchikusha, Tokyo.

Sadler, A. L. *A Short History of Japanese Architecture.* 1941. Reprint. Vermont and Tokyo: Tuttle, 1963.

A classic overview. Parts relating to the *shoin* style are now somewhat dated, but are in general helpful.

Sei, Shonagon. *The Pillow Book of Sei Shonagon.* Translated and edited by Ivan Morris. New York: Columbia University Press, 1967.

The diary of a woman of the Heian court. Includes descriptions of *shinden*-style structures and how they were used.

Shigemori, Kanto. *Japanese Gardens: Islands of Serenity.* Tokyo: Japan Publications, 1971.

A discussion of the major forms found in Japanese gardens, followed by a short historical introduction and sketches of various famous temples.

Statler, Oliver. *Japanese Inn.* Moonachie, N. J.: Pyramid Publications, 1972.

An entertaining work of historical fiction depicting life through the centuries at a high-quality way station much like the former Yakake Inn.

Takeda, Tsuneo. *Kanō Eitoku.* Translated and adapted by H. Mack Horton and Catherine Kaputa. Japanese Arts Library, vol. 3. Tokyo and New York: Kodansha International and Shibundo, 1977.

An in-depth study of the artist responsible for the monumental style of screen painting used in many of the finest *shoin* structures.

INDEX

(glossary not indexed)

245

定価 3,480 円
in Japan